INTRODUCTION

The term "sustainable gardening" is
gardening practices that are not ha
inhabitants and at the same time attem
Sustain and sustenance are defined by the terms "support,"
"preserve," "keep alive," "maintain," "reinforce," and "nutrition." So,
let's look at the gardening practices that encourage sustainability.

Many new gardeners think sustainable gardening is a synonym
for organic gardening. They may be similar in certain concepts, but
not all organic practices are considered sustainable, and vice versa.
Sustainable refers to practices on taking care of your garden without
depleting it of its natural sources all while aiming to also improving
it over time. This could include planting bee-attracting flowers to
maintain the bee population or building a bird feeder to attract birds
that eat pests, so they don't harm your garden plants. Organic refers
to the practices and guidelines being followed for plants, planting and
how they are maintained. An organic gardener tends to their plants
by providing them with an environment to flourish with components
that are labeled "organic". This consists of seeds, soil, fertilizer, and
pesticides. Organic gardens are created to help the natural use less of
the "unnatural" materials for gardening. Sustainable gardening
attempts to use the land, the earth without harming it and its
components.

A sustainable gardener might attempt to improve their gardens
using organic methods, but they might also resort to some not-so
organic means if they are at odds with their goals. They might, for
example, use pesticides or other chemicals if those methods will work

1

better in the long run. To be considered truly sustainable, your garden must not only be able to survive but thrive even in less than perfect conditions. This may mean that you continually monitor your garden and troubleshoot when necessary and then change aspects until you find the sweet spot. Gardening is more an art with some Science, more than the other way around. As with anything, what may work for one, may not work for another. The point is continuous improvement for maximum benefit.

Since sustainable gardening is a philosophy and not an exact science, its meaning has many different interpretations. No two sustainable gardens are the same because no two gardeners grow the same way.

Sustainability is about increasing your garden's natural resources and eliminating waste. The goal of a sustainable gardener is to make their garden self-sufficient and create as little waste as possible.

This type of gardening attempts to mimic eco-systems to allow the plants to thrive. Sustainable gardeners often use mulches or composts as a good way to "return" nutrients to the soil. Composts are made by combining organic materials such as leaves, manure, and kitchen scraps with water and decompose over time into usable plant food. The compost is used as an addition to the soil for the plants' roots to access this nutrient rich resource. Mulches are organic material used around the base of plants instead of grass or another ground cover; they slow erosion, conserve water, add nitrogen back into the soil and modify the soil's pH level making it more acidic or alkaline depending on the plant's needs.

SUSTAINABLE GARDENING FOR THE COMPLETE BEGINNER

FROM SEED TO HARVEST FOR APARTMENT

GARDENING TO BACKYARD

HOMESTEADING

By:

LD Greens

Table of Contents

A garden that sustains itself with minimal human assistance and uses its resources efficiently without depleting it is what the gardener aims for, thus enabling them to rely on it. In nature, a tree would not need care if it was self-sufficient and able to find enough water, sunlight, and nutrients in its habitat and would not require pesticides or herbicides. This ideal garden can be achieved by using methods that mimic the natural processes of an ecosystem while expanding to meet needs. In a non-sustainable setting, most plants will have their very life depended on human oversight and intervention, whereas a sustainable garden will require only minimal ongoing care and maintenance.

What then is a sustainable gardening method? This method continually improves the environment or uses the least number of outside resources to get the most out of the earth and land. In other words, it does not deplete its resources, kills no animals, or plants for food, and leaves behind no waste. This entails finding ways to feed your plants without harming other living things, such as creating compost that allows beneficial microorganisms to live in your soil, so you don't have to buy fertilizer now or ever again. It might also mean planting plants that are low maintenance and self-sustaining, attracting animals who will snack on pests, and attracting insects and creatures that are beneficial to your garden! Gardeners are using these sustainable gardening methods to get the same result that an ecosystem would naturally use.

A sustainable garden is mostly low maintenance. The garden should have no unnecessary chemicals or pesticides on its leaves, stems, and roots. It must have a water source that replenishes itself if your settings and set ups allow for it. The gardener, not having to do much intervening in the long run other than keeping the grounds clean and healthy. The plants should also withstand bad weather so they will not wilt from drought or freeze from frost in winter which may kill plants if not prepared correctly.

In the end, the goal is to have a garden that supplies your family with healthy, locally grown food for the entire year. This can be done in an intensively cultivated small plot or a wide-open lawn or a vast land. Suitable locations are everywhere, and some can even be found in backyards. A very large garden to produce as much food as you need throughout the year is not essential. Follow your whim as to how much or how little you want to do this. Remember, this is *YOUR* garden. *YOU* must enjoy the whole process while having a very positive impact to the society and your environment! Sustainable gardening is more about principle than quantity, and you can get started today with any garden plot of any size. Your garden can be whatever you make it, and it will be sustainable. You need to be the one that will make it happen.

Your decision on what goes into your garden must also be sustainable, thus must stack up in the long run. Do not use unsustainable resources or use up more than you can replenish. What goes into your garden will best serve its purpose if components have multiple functions. Careful planning of what plants to use and what plants to go along with them is one example of this concept.

A sustainable garden will provide food, water, and shelter for other organisms. It flourishes even with the least amount of input, and this is achievable by careful and proper planning. The work you do will pay off in the long term.

CHAPTER 1: PLANNING YOUR GARDEN

One of the best parts of sustainable gardening is the ability and the capacity of starting a garden anywhere. Whether you live in an apartment or a homestead, there is always an opportunity for you to grow your own food, even if your lifestyle doesn't allow for much physical space in your home. If you have a lawn, patio, or balcony, then you have room to grow some food. Wherever your location, there is a way to create and maintain a garden.

Planning your garden is one of the most important parts of gardening. You want to think about how much space you need to grow all the food you want and need. You also want to consider what type of soil you have, how much sunlight will hit your garden, and if you have any other plants growing nearby that might impact your own.

It would be beneficial if you considered the amount of space available and the location of your garden. This book will help you find the best way that works for you. You will want to make sure that you know what type of gardening is right for you and your lifestyle.

Things that you need to consider when it comes to finding space for your garden

1. The space you have

How large will your garden be? If you have a balcony, patio, lawn, or maybe the ground outside of your home, you need to make sure that you know how much space to put aside for your garden.

2. The location of your garden

If you live in an apartment and have a small balcony or lawn outside of your home, then you can maximize and do everything in that small space. However, if you live in a farm or a ranch with plenty of room extending into the large backyard and surrounded by trees and other plants growing around it, then it would be best to consider something that will utilize the space efficiently. It would be beneficial to consider your available space and the location of your garden.

3. Tasks you want to do

If you are going to do everything on your own, you should consider whether this is a good fit for your lifestyle. If you aren't too fond of doing hard labor, consider getting help or finding a different way that requires less work. You can always find ways to help focus on the more essential things in your life.

4 Time and effort

Gardening takes a significant amount of work and care, so along with planning your garden, also consider amount of time and energy you are willing to put in and decide what kind of plants that will thrive in the specified amount of time you decide on.

5. Supplies that you need

Which type of garden are you going to cultivate? Are you growing vegetables, having a flower garden, or doing something else? Every kind of gardening requires different supplies ranging from seeds and other planting necessities to specialized tools needed for each type. Find an option for gardening that works for your lifestyle. It may require a lot of unique supplies, or details but what is important is it is something that will serve your needs.

6. How much time and energy you are going to give to it

You can start small, and compound from there, or go big and check off all necessary steps in one go. However, you decide to do it, make sure it is something that you can sustain and will be a key to the success of your garden. However, the good news is that if you put things in place and you chose sustainable practices, time needed to tend to your garden will be far less in the long run. If you look through all the options presented in this book, you will find something that fits your lifestyle better that may not require as much work.

7. The plants that are right for your space

Are there plants already growing on your property? If so, you can use these plants to start with because they probably won't overgrow into your garden space. If you do have trees, shrubs, and other plants already growing on your property, then you will have to consider if they can be modified or moved around so that you can create a space for your garden.

8. How much sunlight does your space receive

Are you aware of the amount of sunlight that your garden will receive? If it doesn't get a lot of light and is in the shadows of other buildings or trees, perhaps you should move to another place where it will get more sun or create a different plan for the garden. This is an essential option because, without enough sunlight, your plants won't grow as well as they should. Either this or opt for indoor gardening which utilizes grow lights.

9. How you are going to get into your space

Accessibility is crucial. If it is on a balcony or a small apartment, simply making sure that you have access and room for your garden is enough. However, if it is on the ground and surrounded by other plants and trees that block your access to the plants, making sure you can easily get to your plants in your garden and make things easier for you. Always think long term.

10. What type of soil do you have

Are you aware of the type of soil in which your garden will be planted? If it is dirt, sand, gravel, or rock, instead of your garden having raised beds or composted soil, or composted manure or composted peat moss, then you will want to consider changing the plan for your garden. Raised beds hold their nutrients and are easily modified if necessary.

Determining these decisions in the beginning is essential to ensure that gardening will be greatly beneficial and fun!

CHAPTER 2: BACKYARD (OUTDOOR) GARDENING

This is gardening done in the backyard, whether in the ground or raised beds. Some people have chosen to put theirs in containers, while others have put them on top of their patios or back porches. This gardening can be fun and exciting because you can get some fresh herbs that you can use for cooking, a small flower garden for your front porch or patio, or even a vegetable garden for your dinner table. It would help decide how much space you want to dedicate to your garden and what types of things you want to grow.

Which Gardening Style is best for you?

Knowing how much space you need will help you figure out how big your garden should be, while the type of gardening you want to do will determine where in the yard to plant your garden. There are a few types of gardening techniques you can choose from:

Raised beds

Raised beds are small wooden boxes usually made of lumber. They are straightforward to use if you would rather not have a lot of dirt going into your garden bed. Put the wooden planks inside the box and fill it with compost, soil, sand, or peat moss. Once you prepare it properly, you can grow just about anything in this garden bed. You can easily convert this plan for a vegetable garden into one for flowers, herbs, or decorative plants as well. When we refer to a "raised garden bed" or simply "raised bed," we're referring to a freestanding box or frame—traditionally without a bottom or top—that sits aboveground in a sunny location and is filled with high-quality soil. Raised beds are typically open on the bottom to allow the roots of the plants to reach nutrients below ground level. There are also the kind of boxes where the planter is designed to be off the ground, mainly used for smaller growth plants. This is also helpful to maximize your space and helps to prevent the need to bend to reach your plants, saving your knees and your back.

Advantages of Raised Garden Beds

1. Easy to build and require little labor

You can significantly save money if you build it yourself. If you decide to purchase one ready-made, it can also be very affordable. This is a popular idea for many people because it is easy to get a small one set up in your backyard, and then you can expand as necessary. This is an excellent option for those with limited space who don't have the time or energy to put it into a big garden. Growing a small container garden can be manageable for many people specially in apartments and doesn't require as much work as a traditional backyard in soil gardening.

2. It is simple and easy to maintain

You won't have to do much work over the summer or year-round, and it will save you a lot of time. You don't have to weed the soil or plant new seeds every year. You can place it on your porch or patio with a small container and enjoy growing it.

3. It is suitable for beginning gardeners.

Raised beds aren't nearly as complicated or technical as a big garden, making it suitable for beginners to get started and learn new things. Even if you have been gardening before, a raised bed lets you try something new without worrying about the entire garden dying off at the end of the season.

4. Space-saving

Because it is built aboveground, it provides more space for growing your plants than a garden in the ground would because it utilizes vertical space. It allows you to grow more than just a small herb or flower garden.

5. Easy for even for those with limited abilities

It doesn't require high levels of physical strength, making it very useful for those with limitations in abilities as they can work easily in their gardens. It's simple to set up and use, allowing you to grow as many plants as you want in your space while still having a safe place to put them all.

6. It is easy to start from scratch

You don't have to worry about the soil breaking up by turning the dirt. You can fill the bed with soil and compost and start growing your plants.

7. You can grow more than one type of plant in a single area

Because it is built aboveground, you can plant different kinds of vegetables, herbs, or flowers all in one place and have them grow together nicely. This saves space and helps you use all your garden's potential for producing food for you.

8. It conserves water

Because the plants are aboveground, they get more sunlight. The roots won't die due to drowning. This allows you to grow your plants with less water and makes it an eco-friendlier option.

9. It provides a more stable ground for your plants

Your plants don't need to worry about sinking into the ground. This protects your roots from damage, so you can take advantage of everything that your garden can do for you.

10. It is a very natural option to use

You can grow your plants aboveground without worrying about making them look very formal. This lets it look simple and understated, which can make all the difference in how your garden looks and improves its total aesthetic appeal.

Disadvantages of Raised Garden Beds

1. It is time-consuming and energy-consuming to build

It takes time and energy to make a raised garden bed. Many people think it's expensive to buy a readymade one and prefer to make them from scratch. But it may require a lot of woodwork to put it together—something that might not interest everyone. But, if you are crafty, then this is absolutely for you!

2. It requires a little more upkeep to consider

Living in a hot climate means you must be careful with your plants and make sure they don't get too hot from the sun. In colder weather where in there is not enough absorption of water by the plants, there's a risk of growing mold on the roots and soil.

3. It is not appropriate for all types of plants.

Because the soil is exposed and there is no room for deep roots, it isn't suited for growing root vegetables or other plant types that require a lot of space to grow their roots deep into the soil. Some plants will produce small produce because they don't have much room to grow large.

4. It will not be easy to water the plants if it is not placed correctly.

If you have a raised garden bed with holes at the bottom the water and soil might also drain out of the bed, making it difficult to restore it to its original condition after watering. If you wish to avoid this, you may need to adjust like placing liners at the bottom of your box to prevent the water from drying up too quickly, but also balancing it to not rot due to overwatering.

5. It can become moldy if left wet for too long.

Balance is always key, even in gardening!

How to Make a Raised Bed Garden

The following is a step-by-step guide on making a raised bed garden.

Materials:

- Soil
- Planting mix or compost
- Watering tool
- Garden tools
- seedlings

Step 1: Choose the site where you want to build your raised bed garden.

It should be a sunny spot and away from trees, bushes, or anything that would overhang. If the area is very windy, plan on building a windbreak or fence to protect your plants from the wind. The best size for a raised bed is about 4 ft x 8 ft. You can make each side any length you want if it is greater than 2' in height. Ensure that the dimensions fit your selected area and not go over anything (i.e., a fence line).

Step 2: Building Your Garden Bed
Tools

- Drill/driver and bits, screwdriver
- If cutting the planks, yourself (vs. lumber store): Hand saw, tape measure

Materials

- For a 4x8 footbed, obtain three 8-foot-long 2"x6" lumber pieces. It is even better if they have 2"x8" or 2"x10" lumber. Two pieces of lumber will suffice for a 4x4 bed.
- It is best to ask the guys at the lumberyard to cut the pieces in half for you. For the 4x8 footbed, cut one of the pieces in half, leaving two 4-foot lengths for the ends. Cut both pieces in half for the 4x4 bed.
- Screws for the deck/exterior
- To reinforce it, use a 2X4 or 4X4 in the corners to provide a stable surface for nailing or screwing rather than the board's end grain.
- You can place a mesh layer at the bottom of your raised bed to maintain the soil layer

Step 2.1. Make the Bed Sides

1. If your two eight-foot-long boards were not pre-cut at the lumber store, mark the halfway point, and cut each plank in half to create a four-foot-by-four-foot bed. After that, you will have four planks (8-foot by 4-foot).
2. Place each half on a plank and measure down 3/4" from each end for two hinges. Secure two hinges to each board using two #6 x 1 1/2" screws, drill them into the board and in through the hinge. Ensure the hinge and screw are not too tight because that will cause your planks to sag over time. If you have a 2x6, 2x8, or 2x10 wood plank that is 8' long, you can safely screw it into place with a bit of patience as well.
3. If you desire additional bracing and a more robust frame, use two 2x6, 2x8, or 2x10 wood planks 1/2" to 3/4" thick and 3-

5' long. Stagger them or place them on a string to ensure you correct spacing. Screw all four sides into the 2x6s and 2x8s. Make sure you don't screw too tightly against the edges of the 2x6 planks, or it could cause splinters in your wood.

Step 3: Fill the Bed

Level the ground at the site of your garden bed and fill it with a soil-based mixture (such as potting soil) to within an inch of the top.

Step 3.1: Water the area thoroughly, making sure to soak down about 4 inches below ground level to prevent air pockets from making your seedlings dry.

Step 3.2: Use a shovel to move the soil into your raised bed.

Step 3.3: If you are filling a decked raised bed, place one of the four-feet-by-four- feet planks on top of it and serve both sides around it as much as possible.

Step 3.4: Use a hand watering tool to ensure that the soil is soaked.

Step 3.5: Rake all the loose soil and even it out.

Step 3.6: Build up your bed about two or three inches with soil and water it if you haven't, ensuring no empty pockets are left in the outside layer of dirt. Then, let your garden bed settle for a couple of days before planting or moving your patio set into place so that it has time to settle in.

Step 4: Planting Your Raised Bed

You can now plant in your garden beds any combination of plants that will thrive in your area.

Step 4.1: You can plant directly into the ground or garden bed or shallowly into the soil in pots. As a rule, you should use shallow containers and plants which will not grow deeper than 2 inches deep. Otherwise, it may be necessary to set up a trellis above the plants to support them, or you may have to remove them if they get too tall or may need to move them in ground.

Step 4.2: Fill the planting containers with potting soil to within 2" of the tops.

Step 4.3: Plant your seedlings a

Examples:

1. Tomato Plant
2. Perennial Rose
3. Basil
4. Wheat Grass
5. Peppers or Bell Peppers
6. Radishes
7. Carrots
8. Green Onions or Scallions
9. Lettuce
10. Celery or Celeriac
11. Zucchini (courgette)
12. Melon Plants
13. Cucumber Plants
14. Cabbages
15. Eggplants

An adequately built raised bed garden bed can last for years and will provide you with a bountiful supply of fresh food.

CHAPTER 2.1: THE NO-DIG GARDEN

Reference: https://guardian.ng/saturday-magazine/no-dig-gardening-an-easier-way-to-grow/

In the 1950s, when Victory Gardens were shared, a method of gardening that required no digging was developed. People were encouraged to build raised wood-framed garden beds, with a layer of newspapers on the ground that covered and protected the soil. The newspaper was topped with a layer of mulch such as leaves or grass clippings to keep in moisture and prevent weed growth. Thus, the newspaper "dig-free" garden was born.

The method requires no shoveling and prevents weeds by covering up exposed soil with newspaper (ideally printed using ink made from soybeans). The paper decomposes over time and adds nutrients to the ground. The garden bed is generally made of wood as it resists rot. The form can be replaced every year or two with a layer of new newspaper over the top. The soil underneath the paper is protected from weeds and pests, but the form should be changed after several years to add nutrients back into the ground.

Advantages of The No-Dig Method

- It works well on sloped areas because no digging is required; it gives an even surface for planting and growing healthy plants year after year. It works exceptionally well in any place that doesn't get great sun exposure, such as under trees and along fences.

- No-dig gardens are easy to install, even on a slope. The lower end of the garden is dug out about 2 feet wide and 2 feet deep, then filled with newspaper and mulched. The upper end of the garden is left as it is and mulched. Each year, the soil mix can be placed at the bottom end of the garden to amend it further or used in other areas of your property or yard.

- Commonly grown vegetables such as tomatoes, squash, and peppers do well in no-dig gardens. By simply spacing them 3 to 4 inches apart according to their intended maturation location, they can be planted nearer around each other than they would be in standard rows (i.e., 8" apart for a tomato harvested at around 8" across).

- No maintenance is required; the newspaper/mulch garden can grow forever and only improve with time.

- The deep mulch holds moisture, keeping the soil cool in summer and warm in winter, helping ensure success even in cold climates. The mulch also helps prevent frost heaves from occurring.

- If a garden is constructed to fit under a deck, this method of gardening can be pretty handy as the extra protection from the light provided by the patio makes for perfect growing conditions for your crops, especially if you are short on space (no tilling means you have more room) and will save you the time and effort of digging up your yard.
- Instead of traditional methods that pollute the environment by using heavy machinery and pesticides, the no-dig process is environmentally friendly because it uses no fossil fuels or tools to create a garden in whatever space you have available.
- The no-dig method does not require irrigation, which means no foreign substances are entering your home or yard, allowing for better soils and healthier plants than traditional gardening methods that use fertilizers, pesticides, and lots more chemicals in their process of growing.
- There is no need for weed killers since the deep mulch keeps weeds out.
- Its aesthetically pleasing look, and effortless installation means you can have a healthy garden without the hassle and mess of digging up your yard.

Disadvantages of The No-Dig Method

- It requires a lot of space because it uses newspaper to cover up the ground. For the soil to be covered by the mulch, newspapers must be placed on top of the earth. This means that for various plants to be grown, one must have a lot of space.
- Weeds grow underneath the mulch, though this is easily remedied by pulling out weeds as they appear or by using a

tiller on an area that has plenty of excess newspaper material on hand.

- It requires a lot of mulch materials and money initially, and it is not easy to pull out plants that are already growing. Though this method is generally easier than hand digging, it does require a tremendous amount of time and effort in the beginning.
- To plant another variety of plants in the same area, one must start all over again with the newspaper at the bottom, adding mulch as they go along until all the gardens are filled up to put plants in.
- Finally, the no-dig method is generally only appropriate for growing small, non-fruiting plants such as peas, lettuce, or radishes.

How to Build a No-Dig Garden

Materials:

1. Mulch. Cloth and newspaper work well, though not recommended. Wood chips work too, primarily when used with newspaper and straw. Multiply the square footage by 80 to get the amount of material needed to cover an 80 square foot garden bed. (An area of 800 square feet, for example, necessitates 160 cubic feet.)
2. Tools. A shovel and a wheelbarrow are all you'll need to get the job done.
3. Enough space for your garden. Square foot gardens are generally 5 feet long and 4 feet wide, though you can make them any size you want.

4. Organic plant material to fill the garden with, like seeds or seedlings.
5. Pencil and paper for drawing out your design.

Preparing the Beds:

Step 1: Level the area you want to create your garden.

This can be done by hand or with a power tiller, depending on the size of your garden. It is unnecessary to level the whole area; select where you want your garden and then level it out by hand.

Step 2: If desired, add compost to the soil before or after planting your veggies.

The compost will release nutrients into your soil and help plants grow faster.

Step 3: Dig out any exposed dirt on the surface of your garden area.

This step is optional, depending on how much loose dirt you have over your garden area. Leave as much loose dirt as possible in place to aid in moisture retention and to shield the soil from direct sunlight during the hot summer months.

Step 4: Dig out any loose dirt in your flower beds, lawn, walkway, and other areas around your home.

This step may be necessary if you don't want your plants to grow too closely together, as the no-dig method is designed to keep plants spaced at least 3 to 4 inches apart by average soil growth. However, if there isn't much dirt on top of the garden soil and it has been previously cultivated to prepare it for planting, you can let it stay in place, so it won't pose a problem.

Step 5: Start covering the soil.

Lay down newspapers, grass clippings, or any materials you have on hand to cover the soil. Outline your beds and plant locations by marking them with a pencil as you go along. If you want to plant in your existing flower bed or lawn, be sure not to put too much material down as it could make things muddy.

Step 6: Add mulch on top of the newspapers/grass clippings.

The amount of mulch needed will vary depending on how thickly you cover your garden area. If you prefer, you can substitute wood chips or wood shavings for the newspaper and grass clippings in this step.

Step 7: Plant your seedlings

Ensure to water appropriately after initial transplanting

Step 8: Add additional compost and mulch every couple of months to help maintain moisture levels in your garden beds.

Once the seeds have germinated, you should remove them from the germination medium you used and cover the beds with the earth instead—this will provide better drainage by preventing the water from sitting on top of the soil instead of penetrating it.

The plants can be replaced every year with new plants—a good time to replace them is after harvesting your crops.

Plants You can Plant in a No Dig Garden

1. Alfalfa
2. Artichokes
3. Beans
4. Beets
5. Broccoli

6. Brussel Sprouts

7. Cabbage

8. Carrots

9. Cauliflower

10. Cherries

11. Corn

12. Cucumber

13. Eggplant

14. Kale

15. Leeks

16. Lettuce

17. Melon

18. Okra

19. Onions, Scallions, Garlic, and Fennel

20. Peas and Beans (Blackeye, Snap, Snow)

21. Peppers (Sweet and Hot)

22. Potatoes (Yukon Gold)

23. Rutabaga (aka Swede or Yellow Turnip)

24. Spinach

25. Squash (Zucchini)

The no-dig gardening method is a great way to start a garden, even if you live in an urban area. Keeping the ground on your plots of land with least external factors means that they can be used for years, saving you money and effort because the dirt will not have to be tilled or maintained annually like in other methods. Many people do not want to use their yards for gardening because of the mess associated with digging up the soil; however, there is no digging involved at all with this method. This means less work and more time for you to relax or spend doing other activities in your yard.

The no-dig gardening method is a relatively new way of planting vegetables, so less research has been done regarding its long-term effects; however, most research indicates that it does not harm the garden area at all.

CHAPTER 2.2: DIG METHOD GARDENING

Dig Method is when you dig up an existing garden to prepare it for planting. The soil is tilled and then covered with a layer of mulch before planting new seedlings and seedlings; the mulch will prevent weeds from growing until the new plants are established and start to grow on their own. This is a very effective method because the soil will retain more water by not compacting, and you won't have to do any weeding or maintenance. Some people think it's hard to find fresh soil for the garden; this method overcomes this problem.

Advantages of Dig Method

- Improves soil structure and water retention, promoting better plant growth.
- Protects against weeds.
- No need to till or maintain, making it much easier to stay healthy and produce the best quality food you can.
- While digging up an existing garden may leave a large root mass exposed near the surface of the soil, this will decompose entirely within a few years, leaving no trace of any of your work.
- Digging up an existing garden is a great way to recycle and use old soil in your new garden area.
- Having an already established garden may reduce the cost of starting a new one, depending on where you live.

Disadvantages of Dig Method

- Depending on your location, the soil may be scarce. This method can be very time-consuming and require a lot of repetitive work.
- Digging up old gardens is not always possible, especially if your yard has never had a garden before.
- For those in urban areas, the cost of getting rid of the old soil may be more than your budget allows. This method is not very practical for apartment complexes or condominiums.

No-dig gardening is an excellent method for starting a garden because it eliminates weeds and makes it much easier to plant seeds or seedlings directly into the ground.

How to Use the Dig Method

Step 1: Dig up your existing garden.

This step is time-consuming, so it's best to begin in early spring when the days are longer, and the ground can dry out quickly. It is also ideal to dig on a dry day, as this will make it easier for you to search and prevent puddles from forming after you're done. The depth of your garden will depend on what kind of plants you want to grow; while most vegetables need only 6 inches of soil, larger plants such as squash or tomatoes may need deeper trenches that are anywhere from 12 to 18 inches deep. The actual depth of your garden should be determined by what you want to grow.

Step 2: Add compost to improve the soil structure and increase its water holding capacity.

If you skip this step, your soil's ability to retain and hold water will deteriorate, making it difficult for your plants to survive. The nutrients in the compost will help maintain your soil's pH, which is essential for all plants.

Step 3: Lay down a layer of mulch over the soil (this can be straw, wood chips, hay, or any other kind of organic material you want to use).

This would prevent weeds from growing and keep the ground cool in summer. The thickness can vary depending on the amount of mulch you are using; however, one inch should be enough to prevent weed growth.

Step 4: Add a leafy cover over the mulch.

This will prevent water from evaporating quickly, which can be very important in gardening. You can use any kind of leaves but avoid leaves with needles or thorns because they may damage the new plants when they are planted. It is best to use something easily degradable such as pine needles or straw, and different kinds of plants have different leaf types that are better suited for the purpose; some people prefer to use clover or wildflowers as a layer, while others prefer oak leaves. The final layer should be 3 inches thick to prevent weeds from growing until the new plants are established and develop independently.

Step 5: Water the area evenly to avoid water on your vegetables.

If a watering can is available, use it; if not, a hose should be used. Make sure you water in early spring, right before the first rain, because this is when you will need most of your water. Take note of where the water goes, as it can run downhill and dry out quickly; however, this is not usually a problem if you use mulch or hay as a layer.

There are other ways to cultivate your garden, such as no-dig, and digging up a garden already in place. The difference between these methods is clear; the no-dig method follows a design and planting pattern, while the digging method removes the existing soil and plants new seeds. Both methods are beneficial, allowing for better sweat equity, water retention, and production quality. No-dig gardening provides more time to relax in your yard due to its ease of planting; however, if you have trouble finding new soil for your garden or do not want to dig it up from another place, then digging up an existing garden might be a better choice. Both methods will require some time and effort, but that is unavoidable when gardening, as each method requires some work. Taking care of your garden will pay off later, as you will be able to grow fresh vegetables on your own.

The time and effort necessary to manufacture new soil distinguishes the no-dig gardening method from the dig method gardening. The benefit of the dig method gardening is that it is already prepared and needs only a few adjustments to get it in working order. This is not true for the no-dig gardening method because it requires a significant amount of work and patience before you can begin planting. The dig method gardening needs no preparation beforehand, as it can be found in every garden, making it the perfect choice for those unable to dig or have difficulty doing so. The dig method gardening is also suitable for people who want to recycle old soil and shrink their lawn size, which can be more difficult with the no-dig process. The dig method gardening is best for people who do not have the time or patience to prepare a new bed and have already found where their garden will grow.

The no-dig planting method can only be used in certain situations because it requires specific materials that aren't always available. The dig method gardening can be used anywhere, so it is the best option for people who are okay with doing some work before planting. This method needs no preparation beforehand and can be found in every backyard, making it suitable for those who have difficulty digging or finding new soil for their garden.

It might take a little bit of time for your garden to get established and start growing, but once the plants are up and growing, the amount of time required to care for them is drastically reduced. Depending on how much work you had to do to get your garden or soil ready, you may only need twenty-five percent of the time spent, if you choose this method. Both methods can be used simultaneously, so there's no need to choose one; they are compatible and suitable for different people. It all depends on your preference.

CHAPTER 3: APARTMENT (SMALL SPACE OR INDOOR) GARDENING

You should grow plants even if you live in a small apartment. In addition to common houseplants, an apartment garden can support a variety of herbs, fruits, and vegetables.

Apartment living does not necessitate a diet devoid of fresh fruits and vegetables. You can grow a garden by planning and using containers or a small area in the apartment.

An apartment garden can be as small as a single herb pot on the kitchen windowsill or as large as several dozen containers that take up most of the balcony. You can still grow your vegetables indoors, no matter what size your space is.

Things to Consider in Indoor Gardening

While some plants are more forgiving and hardier for novice gardeners than others, all plants have specific growing requirements that must be met.

Consider the following factors when choosing plants for your apartment garden:

1. Sunlight

A full day of sunlight is required for most fruiting and flowering plants. This translates into approximately six to eight hours of direct sunlight per day. This can be difficult in an apartment, and it can be even more difficult if you live in a tri-level apartment or in a high-rise building. If you're gardening on a windowsill, you have two options:

choose plants that require less sunlight, such as salad greens and herbs, or use a grow light to simulate the sun's rays.

2. Temperature

No matter what plants you select, the temperature in your home can affect your plant's growth. Indoor gardens are usually kept in a warm environment to encourage healthy plant growth, but significant shifts in temperature will stress the plant and prevent it from thriving. You should find an area that stays relatively warm throughout the day and keeps cool at night. In the summer, you may wish to use a small fan to help circulate air and prevent your plants from becoming too hot during the day.

3. Wind

Gardens placed on balconies or near open windows can easily be affected by wind, especially if you live near an area with solid breezes or frequent storms. Although most plants can handle some level of wind, the constant movement will stress them and possibly prevent them from flowering or fruiting.

4. Light

Most plants require a certain level of light to grow properly. If you're using artificial light, such as fluorescent or LED grow lights, you'll need to consider the intensity of your light compared to sunlight, so your plants get the right amount of light they need to stay healthy. Plant leaves will turn yellow and become deformed if you use too much or too little. Adjusting the height of your plants can also help you direct light toward them.

5. Water

Plants need water to live. However, too much water will drown your plants, so it's essential to know how much they need. A general recommendation is to keep the soil moist but not soaking wet. If the ground is full of stagnant water, this will cause root rot and damage your plants. It would help if you always let containers sit in a bowl of water for a few hours after watering them every few days. This allows the roots to absorb more moisture and prevents excess water from being lost to evaporation. Some plants like cacti and succulents prefer drier conditions, so it might be helpful to use pots with a small amount of soil when watering your garden indoors.

6. Soil

Plants won't grow without soil. Select a type of soil that is right for your plant's needs. If you're new to gardening, use a simple mixture of compost, sand, peat moss, or vermiculite to create a potting mix for your garden. You can also buy small bags of soil from your local garden center or hardware store.

7. Humidity

Humidity is a factor you'll need to consider when growing indoor garden plants. Plants in pots will experience much less moisture than their outdoor counterparts, but they need the same amount of humidity to stay healthy. Keeping them at proper humidity allows roots to absorb water quickly and prevents fungus and disease. If your apartment doesn't have adequate ventilation, it might be helpful to use an oscillating fan on low or medium settings during hot days.

8. Containers

Plants can grow in various containers, including pots (live plants), plastic containers, baskets, and hanging baskets. Use the right size containers for your plants. A plant grown in a small pot will have cramped roots and probably won't grow as large as it would in a larger pot. Fill the container with your potting soil and make a hole for each plant you want to transplant. Many containers also come with holes already in them, making this job even more accessible.

9. Weight

When filled with multiple plants, containers can become quite heavy and difficult to move around. Assemble a container garden that's lightweight and easy to carry. This will make tending to your plants even more accessible. If you're using larger pots, place them on a sturdy surface where they won't slide around or fall over.

10. Space

The space available in your apartment or room can limit or expand the size of your garden. You may need to adjust for large plants like trees and vines, which can quickly take up a lot of space. You can prune these back often to keep them from growing too large for small spaces.

You've found the perfect place for your apartment garden, but will you have enough space to keep all your plants happy? This cannot be easy. You want a space that allows you to water and care for the plants properly, but you don't want to waste valuable floor space on dead or dying plants.

Which gardening style is best for you?

There are many different gardening styles to choose from. Some people like to start from scratch and work with a blank slate, while others prefer to work with nature by working with soil already planted by someone else. Most people find a happy medium between the two and add flavor to their garden.

Container gardening

Reference: https://www.mahealthyfoodsinasnap.org/healthy-you/blog/2019/05/29/starting-your-indoor-container-garden

By filling pots, tubs, and half barrels with flowers, container gardening can add appeal to any garden, but it can also serve a practical purpose. Container gardening is an excellent option for those who don't have a lot of garden space.

Advantages of Container Gardening

1. It Helps Make the Most of Limited Space

Because containers can be stacked, and easily moved around, gardeners can use their limited space in the most efficient way possible. Container gardens also allow plants with a wide range of height to be grown together.

2. It Allows for Increased Control Over Watering Needs

Gardeners who have problems (either overwatering or under watering) often choose container gardening as a viable option. Containers are easy to move towards a sink or hose faucet, allowing the gardener to water when needed while still controlling how much water goes into the container.

3. It Has Fewer Insects and Diseases

Since container plants have limited space and thin, sparse root systems, they have fewer insect and disease problems.

4. It Allows for Easy Transportation

Container gardening enables you to easily relocate your garden. This allows the gardener to take their garden indoors during the cold winter months or outdoors for a barbecue party in the summertime.

5. It is Versatile in Design Styles

Container gardens can be designed with various styles from country cottage to formal Victorian or even modern minimalist with ease. The possibilities are endless.

6. It Allows the Gardener to Create a Theme by Growing Plants to Match Their Lifestyle

Container gardens are an excellent way for gardeners to express themselves by growing plants that match their lifestyles, hobbies, or interests. Perhaps you're decorating your apartment in an Asian theme, and you want a plant that reflects that. Container gardening is also an excellent way for gardeners to grow edible plants on the patio or balcony instead of leaving those containers bare in between cookouts and barbeques.

7. It reduces maintenance

Container gardening reduces maintenance time by allowing you to move your plants farther away from dirt and lawn when mowing is necessary.

8. Aesthetics

Container gardening allows you to display your crops or flowers in the house without ruining the visual appeal of your surrounding area. It is also one way people decorate their yards while keeping it practical (since containers can easily be moved around).

9. It requires less maintenance

Since you're growing in a container, your plants only need soil, water, and nutrients to thrive rather than being buried under natural soil, mulch, and rainwater collection systems like traditional gardens do. No weeding or other maintenance is required unless you want to grow edible plants or shrubs in pots that are susceptible to pests such as rabbits, squirrels, raccoons, and other invaders.

10. It facilitates small scale gardening

Container plants can be used on decks, patios, balconies, and rooftops, as well as in unused corners of garages and sheds, and even on a small windowsill. The convenience of a container garden also makes it easier to maintain plants when away from home while still keeping your green thumb. Few things make a house as inviting as a well-kept garden.

Disadvantages

1. Limited Space Available in Most Apartments and Homes.

Containers are not nearly enough space to comfortably fit a garden. Apartments and condominiums that have balconies or terraces often use them for planter hampers rather than retaining walls. Some people choose to grow vegetables in the ground and take advantage of the high yield by growing a variety of crops, or even herbs for cooking.

2. It Requires Patience for Longer Growing Times

Gardening in containers limits how large the roots of your plants can grow, so you may have to give up on growing fruit trees if you have a small space.

3. It Requires Proper Ventilation

Container gardening can limit air circulation around the plant, so it's essential to make sure your container garden gets plenty of ventilation during the warmer months. This is especially true in a small apartment or house where you don't have a lot of space to move the containers around.

Container gardening can be considered the most versatile style of gardening. Its versatility, convenience, and flexibility make it a great choice for those who don't have much garden space and need to have their plants stay small enough to fit in spaces that are tight on their own. Container gardening is ideal for growing a variety of plants in the same container, regardless of size. The main drawback of container gardening is the limited space available in most apartments and homes.

Starting Your Indoor Container Garden

1. Choosing the Container

You can use any container that you choose, but it's best to choose a container that is the same size as your plant. It allows you to better control the frequency of watering and the use of herbicides. The most common containers are:

- Plastic buckets
- Half barrels
- Flowerpots
- Large tubs and crates
- Commercial hanging baskets

The main drawback to plastic containers is that they can become brittle and crack over time, making them susceptible to leaks. Also, these containers are often not as attractive as other types of containers, except hanging baskets. The benefit is that they are generally less expensive than their counterparts.

2. Choosing the Plants for Your Container Garden

When you choose a plant for your container garden, it's important to consider what type of growth pattern it will have and how long you want your container garden to last (because some plants will grow for multiple seasons) before you choose the plant.

To name some of the common plants to choose for containers for the sustainable garden:

Flowers that bloom throughout the year

These plants usually have an annual life cycle and can bloom for some time without being planted again. They include:

- Begonias
- Columbines
- Goldenrods
- Ranunculus
- Verbena
- Dahlias
- Marigolds
- Hibiscus

Plants that grow in containers but need to be planted outside

Some plants such as beans and tomatoes are grown bi-annually in their containers because they don't want their roots disturbed when they grow into the container (or because the soil can become too heavy). After the container is discarded, they can be planted in the garden. These include:

- Beans
- Corn
- Garlic
- Potatoes
- Strawberries

Plants that grow best in containers but will grow well outside in the garden

These plants include yucca and succulent plants such as aloes and jade plants. They will generally do well with or without being planted in soil but are usually grown indoors in pots because of their fragile nature. These plants also grow relatively quickly in containers compared to their counterparts on a lawn. These plants include:

- Colocasia
- Crassula
- Cissus
- Echeveria
- Hornwort (Equisetum)
- Crassula
- Podophyllum
- Yucca

Plants that grow well in pots but will grow better in the ground

These include most perennials. Most of these plants will do a better job growing on their soil in the garden and shouldn't be planted directly in a pot. These include:

- Ferns (especially those with large rhizomes)
- Cranberries and blueberries
- Daylilies
- Butterfly bushes

Although they will grow better in the ground, many of these plants can be grown successfully in containers. Some of these plants are not grown as annuals but potted perennials. It's another option to consider when choosing the type of plant, you want to start in your container garden.

3. Making Your Indoor Container Garden

Step 1: Choose the plant that you want to put in the container

To start, it is best to choose one from the list of recommended plants for a sustainable garden. Choose whichever plant interests you the most and isn't subject to overbearing neighbors (such as a large tree). The container garden will have to be transported to an area of the yard or garden before being transplanted.

Step 2: Choose your container for the plant

Choosing a container for your plant is important. The container is an important factor in how long the plant will grow. Repotting will take longer if the container is larger. You will probably want a container at least 4' in diameter and between 8" - 10" deep to get a good yield out of it. A pot should not be too small or large, resulting in poor growth once planted in soil (or even when pot-bound).

Step 3: Determine the size your plant will need

The container's size depends on how big the plant will grow. Take into consideration how many plants you want to put in the container. Also, consider your container's size or whether you have enough space for a bigger container. To avoid being limited by space constraints, choose a size that will fit comfortably into your containers. It's possible that you'll have to try a few different containers before finding one that works well with the plant you want to start it in.

Step 4: Decide on the type of soil you want to put in the container

Choose a soil that is suitable for your plant. Use a standard potting mix with lots of organic matter for all plants. For large crops (such as corn and potatoes), use 1/2 peat and 1/2 vermiculite or perlite.

Use a standard potting mix with no fertilizer for smaller vegetables like tomatoes, peppers, and herbs.

Step 5: Decide on the placement of the container.

Choose the best location for your container. Consider how simple it will be to maintain, how much light it will receive, and whether it will require additional water. Ensure that you don't place containers directly in the sun or close to heat sources or vents (such as electrical outlets). The location of your container also needs to be clear of large areas that are prone to flooding.

Step 6: Water and plant

Water the plant and the soil, then place the plant in its container. Place your container in a sunny area or under a grow light. If you use a grow light, make sure that it is no less than 2 feet from the leaves of your plants (if using fluorescent lights). Regularly inspect your plant for growth and treat any insects that appear to prevent them from causing serious damage.

Containers can be a useful tool for any home gardener, allowing you to start your plants from seed or cuttings and transplant them into the ground when they are sufficiently grown. There are numerous advantages to container gardening, and these advantages can be used to create a sustainable garden.

CHAPTER 3.1: VERTICAL GARDENING

Reference: https://www.pinterest.com/pin/645492559075825329/

Vertical gardens are an excellent option for gardeners who lack horizontal space, want to conceal an unsightly wall, or simply want something different. Apartment dwellers, small-space urban gardeners, as well as gardeners with large, traditional spaces, can benefit from vertical gardening with upright structures. Small-stature houseplants can be grown indoors to create a garden in a container or on walls and can be hanging.

Advantages of Vertical Gardening

1. Upright structures provide easier access to all parts of the garden.

2. Upright structures can be used as dividers in a larger garden or indoor space, letting you use a small percentage of the available space.
3. In vertical gardens, plants can grow on walls and ceilings instead of sitting in pots on floors. This way, your plants have an unobstructed view and sunlight that walls or other furniture items can't filter.
4. Vertical gardening is handy for small spaces because it takes less equipment than container gardening and less space than traditional gardening methods (soil, plants, and water are compacted into smaller spaces).
5. Vertical gardens make growing plants such as flowers, herbs, fruits, and vegetables easy.
6. Vertical gardening is more environmentally friendly because it doesn't require soil, fertilizer, and water supplies.
7. Upright structures can be easily built in many different styles or colors.

Disadvantages of Vertical Gardening

1. Depending on the size, vertical gardens are more expensive than other gardening options (pots, benches, and containers). Additionally, prices vary based on the quality of the construction materials used; low-quality materials will not last long enough to justify the related maintenance costs.
2. Vertical gardens are generally limited to growing plants in containers due to few structural options.

Although there are a few disadvantages to vertical gardening, the advantages greatly outweigh them. By purchasing an upright structure and using it to grow your plants, you can save money, create a beautiful space, grow a wide variety of plants, and create a healthy environment for your plants.

Starting an Indoor Vertical Gardening

Step 1: Choose the right vertical structure.

There are many kinds of vertical structures that you can purchase, such as benches and tables and shelves. However, the way the structure is built is key. For example, there are built-in shelves that allow vertical space for plants without any added cost or maintenance. You can also choose from various organic materials like bamboo and bamboo poles to construct your indoor garden.

Step 1.1: If you use a wall for a vertical garden and get only four hours of sunlight a day, you'll probably want to grow plants that can grow in lower light levels rather than those that require lots of light.

Step 1.2: If you plan to build your garden vertically, you will need to find a way to secure your upright structures or structures that can handle vertical action (plant stands). You can use brackets or adhesive glue designed for wall surfaces.

Step 2: Determine the types of plants you want to grow, considering the amount of space you have, the amount of sunlight available in your area, and your budget.

Before starting your garden, you'll need to decide what type of plants you want to grow. The best option is determined by the size and style of your vertical structure, as well as the amount of light exposure you have.

For example:

1. Lettuce

Leafy green plants like lettuce need a lot of sunlight, so it would be best to grow them in a natural material like bamboo that allows sunlight through easily.

2. Pepper Plants

Tomato and other pepper plants require an abundance of sunlight, so ensure that your structure is large enough to accommodate the plant and has adequate ventilation. You'll also want to choose a structure that will allow a lot of sunlight to pass through.

3. Fruit Plants

Most fruit plants like strawberries and raspberries require only four or five hours of sunlight a day, so you can use almost any material to build your vertical garden. However, you may need more space in the garden for multiple fruits, depending on what you want to grow there (leaves or vegetables).

4. Herbs

Herbs like basil and dill varieties need a lot of sunlight during the day, so try growing them vertically in your garden. You can also grow other herbs indoors if you don't have enough space for a vertical structure.

5. Other Plants

There are hundreds of plants that you can grow in your vertical garden. If you want to grow them, make sure to choose the right material and purchase the right plant size; most plants also require specific soil nutrients and water drainage systems.

Step 3: Decide on the location of your indoor vertical garden.

You will need to find a place in your house with enough room for your vertical structure. Ascertain that you have sufficient space to position plants and soil media throughout the area where you intend to grow or relocate them to another part of the house if necessary.

1. If you're planning to grow plants in a small space like a kitchen, choose an upright structure with shelves or shelves built into walls; this way, you can save space since there's no need to buy pots and containers.

2. If you want to grow plants in an area with a lot of space, like a living room, you can buy an upright structure and use it as a stand for pots or containers that contain your plants.

3. If you are growing plants on your balcony for easy access, you can use benches and tables to distribute the necessary amount of sunlight around your balcony. You'll need to find a place in your house where they're easily accessible and won't take up too much space.

Step 4: Decide where to place pots and containers to grow your plants.

After choosing the right type of structure for your indoor garden, you will need to choose where to place different containers and pots in your vertical garden. The first step is to decide where plants will go so that you don't get any sunburns or plant diseases.

Step 5: Buy pots and other containers for your indoor vertical garden.

1. Make sure your containers are large enough to support a portion of the root ball without damaging the roots, as well as enough media (soil, gravel, or pebbles) to surround it.
2. Make sure that your pots have enough drainage holes in the bottom so that excess water can quickly drain out of the containers without over-soaking your plant's roots.
3. If you choose to use multiple containers for a single plant, layer them with gravel or pebbles to ensure proper drainage and room for media around the roots.
4. If you plan to grow different plants in different containers inside your vertical garden, choose materials and colors that complement each other; this will help create an aesthetically pleasing vertical garden.
5. For extra drainage, consider opening the bottoms of your pots or containers if you know you will be watering a plant with a lot of moisture.

Step 6: Build up soil media inside your vertical garden.

You will need to buy media to fill the containers with and fill them with the right amount of water.

To ensure the health and growth of your plants, you must also provide adequate drainage so that excess moisture does not become stagnant in the soil media.

There are many types of available soil media for growing indoor vertical gardens.

Some popular examples include:

1. Bamboo chips/bamboo shavings

Bamboo is a material that is most often used in vertical gardens because it is easy to work with and gives plants enough sunlight. There are many brands of bamboo shavings, so choose the one that will complement your plants without damaging them.

2. Eco-earth

This growing media is high in nutrients and minerals, allowing your plants to thrive while taking less effort to grow. It's also a green product, so it has no adverse effects on the environment when you dispose of it after you're done using it.

3. Vermiculite

This is an excellent material for growing plants in vertical gardening plans because it's lightweight and easy to work with compared to other types of media materials like perlite or coco coir; this means that your vertical garden will look as good as new after you bring everything inside at the end of the season.

4. Gravel

This material is cost-efficient and very easy to work with so that you won't have any problems with your plan or your plants when you're finished.

5. Pea gravel

This type of gravel is commonly used in flower beds and gardens, so there's no reason why you shouldn't use it for your indoor vertical garden if you're familiar with how it looks and feels.

Step 7: Prepare your plants for growth.

If you want to grow fruit, flowers, or leafy vegetables in your indoor vertical garden, the first step is to ensure that the soil media is suitable for indoor growing. For example, if you're growing plants like strawberries or lettuces that require a lot of water to stay hydrated as they grow, wait until the soil media has been sitting outside in your structure for at least an hour once it has been prepared (so that it will absorb excess moisture from the air) before placing your plant inside and watering it.

Step 8: Place plants in different containers in the vertical garden structure.

In order to keep your plant's roots healthy, you need to make sure that they have the proper number of media around them so that they can stay moist and prevent oxygen from coming in contact with the roots.

Widen the container openings of your vertical structure so that they're bigger than the root ball of your plants.

1. For small plants, like sprouts or seeds, place one on top of the other with layers of gravel in-between them so that they have a good amount of oxygen and drainage.
2. For larger plants, like tomatoes and strawberries, you can use one container for each plant. If you intend to grow multiple plants in the same container, ensure that the containers are large enough to prevent the plants from touching.

Since vertical gardening is an art, don't get discouraged if your container garden doesn't look perfect the first time you try it. The key to growing successful indoor plants is to have a lot of patience and practice.

CHAPTER 4: HARDINESS ZONE '

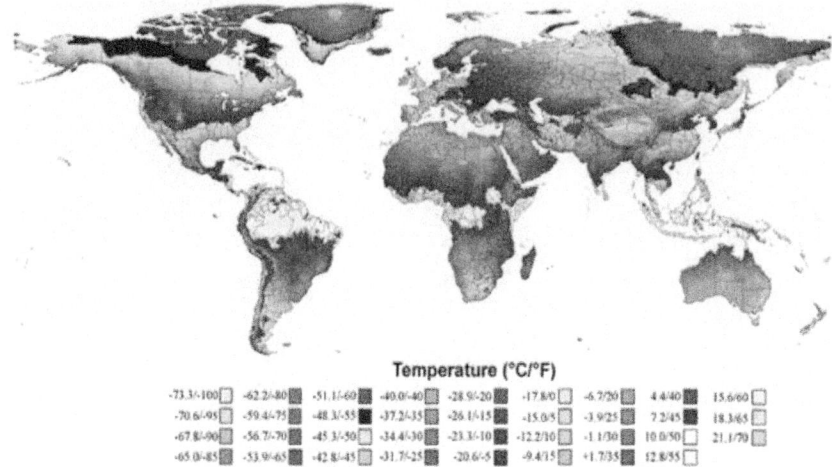

Temperature (°C/°F)

-73.3/-100 ☐ -62.2/-80 ▦ -51.1/-60 ▦ -40.0/-40 ☐ -28.9/-20 ▦ -17.8/0 ☐ -6.7/20 ▦ 4.4/40 ▦ 15.6/60 ☐
-70.6/-95 ☐ -59.4/-75 ▦ -48.3/-55 ▦ -37.2/-35 ☐ -26.1/-15 ▦ -15.0/5 ☐ -3.9/25 ▦ 7.2/45 ▦ 18.3/65 ☐
-67.8/-90 ☐ -56.7/-70 ▦ -45.3/-50 ☐ -34.4/-30 ▦ -23.3/-10 ☐ -12.2/10 ☐ -1.1/30 ▦ 10.0/50 ☐ 21.1/70 ☐
-65.0/-85 ☐ -53.9/-65 ▦ -42.8/-45 ☐ -31.7/-25 ▦ -20.6/-5 ▦ -9.4/15 ☐ +1.7/35 ▦ 12.8/55 ☐

A geographically defined area within which a particular type of plant life can thrive is defined by climatic conditions, including its ability to withstand the zone's minimum temperatures. The zones were initially developed for the United States by the Department of Agriculture (USDA) but have since been adopted by other countries.

The United States Department of Agriculture (USDA) developed the original and most widely used system as a rough guide for landscaping and gardening. It divides the country into 13 zones based on long-term average annual extreme minimum temperatures. It has been adapted in various ways by and for other countries (such as Canada) and is used in climatological studies, plant hardiness, and plant classification.

The original hardiness zone map was developed in the first half of the 20th century by United States Department of Agriculture

(USDA) horticulturalists. USDA researchers recognized that gardening necessitated knowledge about gardening year-round in different areas where different kinds of plants grow well (or do not grow well). They also recognized that although climate changes rapidly throughout the country, summers are relatively stable.

To best determine which plants to include in garden designs and guide new growers toward appropriate sites, they needed a gradually increasing temperature scale with more reliable information than could be gleaned from daily weather reports.

World Hardiness Zones

Most the world's larger countries have their version of a hardiness map. Australia, New Zealand, African countries, Canada, China, Japan, Europe, Russia, and South America use a similar system. However, many have naturally warmer zones, and the zones may extend above the USDA's maximum of 11. Africa countries, New Zealand, and Australia are examples of countries where hardiness zones deviate from the USDA chart. Britain and Ireland are also countries with milder winters than many northern United States. As a result, their map of hardiness zones will range from 7 to 10—Northern Europe experiences colder winters and averages between 2 and 7.

How to Use Hardiness Zone Information

By understanding hardiness zones, you can select plants for your garden that will thrive in your area's winters. The zones are irrelevant for annuals, as these are plants expected to live only during the summer months or one season. For example, a sustainable garden in zone 10 will require planting only native trees and shrubs in the winter.

By understanding which plants can be grown where you can make better choices. For example, if winters are too cold for some plants you'd like to grow, try alternatives that grow well in zones with a 6 or lower. Or, if your gardening budget is limited, consider selecting plants that thrive in zones with a 5 or lower.

Hardiness Zone Converter

To determine the USDA equivalent zone, take the region's average lowest temperature and multiply it by ten degrees for each higher zone. Zone 11 in the United States has an average minimum temperature of 40 degrees Fahrenheit (4 C.). For zones with higher minimum temperatures, such as zone 13, the average minimum temperature is 60 degrees Fahrenheit (15 C.). Naturally, you will need to convert if you live in a region that employs the metric system. Each tenth of a degree Fahrenheit is equivalent to 12.2 degrees Celsius. This hardiness zone converter enables any gardener in any country to determine their hardiness zone, if they know the region's lowest average temperature.

Hardiness zones are important to protect sensitive plants and get the best growth and health out of your sustainable garden. The USDA created the hardiness zone map to help gardeners determine which plants will grow best where they live. Gardeners can use these zones to decide which plants to grow in their gardens and which need not be included. With the help of this map, you can better plan and build a sustainable garden.

Understanding how your garden works is a good thing for the sustainable gardener. Many plant species have different requirements for growth depending on where you are located and what season it is in your area. This chapter has tips on what you can plant when and where to get the most from your landscape.

Even if you are a beginner in sustainable gardening, this information will help you understand how to grow plants at home with the least amount of trouble.

By knowing what kinds of plants can grow in your area, you can select species that thrive in your region's winter temperatures and climate. You can also decide where to plant some types of plants that do not tolerate frost or harsh winters, such as grasses and low-growing flowering bulbs.

CHAPTER 4.1: GARDENING PLANNING FOR YEAR-ROUND PLANTING and HARVESTING

Plant species differ in the best season to plant them, the season they should be planted, and how they grow. The best time to plant most trees and shrubs is in late summer or early fall because this is when trees can produce new roots. Roots mature in late fall through winter, making it easier for them to start growing as soon as spring arrives.

Maybe you feel like the current growing season has passed, and you will need to wait until next spring to start? Or maybe you want to try something new this coming falls or winter? This tip box will help you get started on your new landscape now rather than later.

Season- different seasons, the best time to plant, and what to plant for a sustainable garden

*Disclaimer: This is an estimate as it depends on your area and the specific climate in your area.

Spring

What to Plant:

1. Herbs

Dill, parsley, chives; parsley is best planted in spring as it will continue to bloom all summer and add nice color to the winter season. It's best if you plant it in spring. Be aware that plants are not the same as in other parts of the world. If you plant these plants during springtime, they will rot before winter is over. You can harvest them then or replant them in the fall. Herbs grow as annuals, which means they die after harvesting. It would be beneficial if you planted them early enough in the spring so that they have time to mature before the harsh winter season arrives.

2. Lettuce, spinach, and arugula

These are ideal spring plants as they can be planted in early spring. They are cool-season plants that thrive in weather that is not too hot or too cold. Tender lettuces will bolt and go to seed if the temperature rises above 65 degrees Fahrenheit (18 degrees Celsius). As a result, place them in a shady location. Harvesting this around early summer will give you one season of growth, and then in the fall, you can harvest for a second time.

3. Peas

Peas are ideal for early spring planting in areas with cool springs. While you can plant peas in the fall to harvest in spring, winter-hardy peas should be planted during early spring, as they will not root too well when temperatures drop. Snow peas will root and grow even when planted after a frost. These plants tolerate the cold better than standard garden peas. Snow peas are delicious raw, and they may be steamed or stir-fried with other vegetables or meats. The plants produce edible pods that hold four to six small edible seeds. They are eaten along with the pods when they are young but must be removed before they mature fully so that the plant can continue to grow and produce more pods as they get older.

4. Beans

These crops are very hardy and will thrive under poor growing conditions such as hot sun and poor soil conditions. They are one of the easiest vegetables to grow but can be challenging during harvest. When harvesting, you may want to pluck them out of their vines as soon as you see the first yellow leaves on them so that you do not wait too long before harvesting again, which will make them bitter tasting because they have gone from main season planting to the main harvest at once.

5. Tomatoes

Plant tomato plants in early spring and harvest them when they have reached the size you would like. You can also start seeds indoors. This will give your tomato plants a few extra weeks of growing time before the first frost, which will help them develop a sturdier root system. If you plant tomato seedlings in the ground, put up a cage to protect them from wind and rain. If you leave them out in the open, they are prone to damage from strong winds and heavy rains.

6. Pepper plants

Pepper plants are perennial but can be harvested throughout the growing season until frost in fall and spring. The best time to plant pepper plants is early spring so that they have lots of room to grow before the hot summer months, where they will be prone to attracting bugs. Harvest your first pepper harvest when peppers are around 2 inches (5 cm.) long or when they begin to turn red, depending on what type of pepper you have planted. Pepper plants bloom in late spring/early summer and will produce peppers through the summer.

7. Eggplant

Plant eggplants in early spring and harvest eggplants by the end of summer, often right at the 1-year mark, to get a full season of eggplant production. Eggplants grow best with at least six hours of sunlight a day, particularly if you do not want to keep your plants indoors for the winter months. In addition, they can be grown in a greenhouse.

8. Strawberries

Strawberries prefer cool weather, but they can be grown throughout the year on the ground. Start your seeds indoors in early spring, and plant them outdoors after the last frost and as soon as the soil is workable. Frost will kill off any new strawberry plants, so only plant when you are certain that your area has had all frost for that year to ensure maximum growth. If you grow strawberries in pots, you can grow them inside during the winter months.

9. Melons

Plant melons in early spring, and they will often come back to life in late summer (if you are growing them outdoors). Only plant true cantaloupe and watermelon after the first frost. Plants will stop producing if they receive a frost before they mature. Melons need soil rich in organic matter and well-aerated with ample drainage. They prefer the highest levels of sunlight but can tolerate partial shade. Harvest melons when the fruit is full size or when you see the first blush of color on the plant.

10. Asian squash

These crops are great for growing inside in the winter months. You can also plant fall crops such as beets and carrots to be a fall crop for you to harvest through the rest of summer. Asian squashes can also be grown in raised beds and containers and on the ground. These crops grow well even in poor soil and produce throughout the season until frost.

By planting your crops at different times throughout the spring season, you can ensure a constant harvest. This benefits you because you will never run out of certain vegetables, and it also benefits your garden by giving plants a consistent amount of shade from the hot sun.

Summer

What to Plant:

1. Corn

Plant corn sometime during mid-summer for a fall harvest. You can also plant corn in early spring and then again in late summer for an additional harvest. Corn is a popular summer vegetable crop to plant because it thrives in hot weather and can withstand high temperatures even during periods of drought. However, corn is prone to pests, so make sure that you pay attention to your plants before an infestation occurs.

2. Beans

Beans are best grown in the summer and will germinate for a second harvest during winter if you are lucky enough to have a warm winter. Beans require rich soil and consistent watering, but they are one of the best crops to grow because they can withstand high temperatures and produce for almost an entire year, depending on what type of beans you choose. Beans also fix nitrogen into the soil as they grow, which helps your other plants that would otherwise not get their fair share.

3. Cucumbers

These can be planted at the beginning of summer. They need plenty of water, but not as much as other crops, so give them their fair share of water each day. Cucumber beetles are very bad for cucumbers, so make sure that you watch your plants for any signs of infestation.

4. Potatoes

Potatoes are best planted in fall and then again in late summer. They can produce throughout the winter months, so if you have a cool winter, you can grow potatoes that will be ready to harvest in springtime. The best time to plant potatoes is when they have sprouted but have not yet begun to grow so that they do not take up a lot of space in your garden.

5. Cabbage

Plant cabbage in late summer and then again in the fall for two different harvests throughout the growing season. Cabbage needs consistent moisture to grow well, but it is a very hearty crop that can withstand heat and drought.

6. Lemongrass

Lemongrass grows well in the summer with plenty of sunlight and warm temperatures, but it can also grow throughout the year if you live somewhere that does not get frost or snow. Lemongrass requires very little water to grow, so you do not need to worry about keeping it constantly watered. Lemongrass is a perennial crop that can be harvested throughout the year, even when there is snow on the ground.

7. Okra

Okra is a warm-weather crop that can be planted in mid-summer and again sometime in late summer and early fall for different harvests through the season. Okra is high in nutritional value, and it is a good crop to grow because it can be grown in poor soils. If it grows in excess moisture, okra will produce many seeds, so you will have to thin the plants when they are too crowded.

8. Hot peppers

Plant hot peppers when they are still young and small, and they will grow throughout the entire season with continuous harvests. Hot peppers are very easy to plant, but they need lots of sunlight and warm temperatures to grow well. If you choose not to plant hot peppers in your garden but have a greenhouse or sunroom, keep them there for the summer months.

9. Radishes

Plant radishes in late summer for a fall harvest, or plant them in early summer for harvests in late summer. Radishes require very little water and can tolerate a lot of heat, making them great for gardens with poor soil and limited irrigation resources.

10. Spinach

Plant spinach in late summer, and it will produce for a second time during the fall and winter months. Spinach grows well in sandy soil with very little nutrients, so it is great for less-than-ideal gardens. Spinach needs plenty of water to grow well, so plant it where you can ensure irrigation.

Fall

What to Plant:
1. Carrots

Carrots are a common staple crop for fall harvests throughout the year's cooler months. They can be planted at the beginning of fall and then again toward winter if you live in an area that does not get snow or frost in the winter season. Carrots are a very easy crop to grow because they only take up a lot of space in your garden when they are grown in large bunches.

2. Garlic

Plant garlic in early fall and then again in late fall for a later harvest that will last you through the rest of the winter months. Garlic is one of the most versatile crops to grow because you can use it inside your home for cooking and outside for repelling pests. To prepare garlic for your pantry, simply leave it outside on the ground to dry.

3. Beets

Planting beets in fall will yield a second harvest in the winter months when lots of food is needed. Beets are easy to grow because they need very little water and nutrients, but it will be difficult to keep them from stealing all the nutrients from your other plants. Beets are also a root crop, so if you have fewer resources for growing your garden, beets will survive and thrive.

4. Raspberries

Raspberries are perennial plants that grow best during the fall months when warmer weather returns after the first frost of winter. Raspberries are very sweet and produce lots of juice, so they are great to grow in areas that do not get a lot of nutrients. Raspberries can be grown inside or out, and they also tend to be disease-free, making them a perfect crop that needs very little maintenance.

5. Pumpkins

Pumpkins can be planted in late summer for a fall harvest or in early fall for a winter harvest. Planting in late winter will produce pumpkins for other hungry gardeners throughout the spring and summer months. Pumpkins are easy to grow, but they take up quite a bit of space in your garden and need plenty of nutrients and water to thrive.

6. Kale

Planting kale in fall will produce for a second time during the winter months when lots of food is needed. Kale is a dark green leafy vegetable that produces throughout the year with minor harvest gaps between late summer and early fall. Kale grows best in cool climates, but it can also be grown indoors throughout the year to give you a constant supply of leafy greens.

7. Collard greens

Plant collard greens at the beginning of fall and again during the winter months. for two harvests per season Collard greens are easy to grow and only require very little water to survive, even though they grow best in sandy soil with few nutrients. Collard greens are also a very nutritious green that makes a great choice for gardeners who want to harvest their crops year-round.

8. Chard

Chard is another spinach-like leafy vegetable that grows well in cool climates, but it needs more nutrients and water to thrive than other leafy greens like kale. Plant chards in the fall and then again in the winter months when your areas are not as warm. Chard can be purchased already washed, so you can just remove the tough outer leaves to reveal their true beauty and benefit of the second harvest year-round.

9. Swiss chard

Swiss chard is a leafy vegetable that grows in almost any soil type and is tolerant of extreme temperatures, making it an excellent choice for gardeners with limited resources. Swiss chard can be planted in the fall, but it will not produce seeds, so you will have to separate the plants when they are too crowded. This spinach-like vegetable is another one that is easy to grow, only needing little water and nutrients to survive throughout the entire season.

10. Turnips

Turnips are good crops to plant in early fall as an alternative crop for your winter garden. Turnips are very easy to grow, but they require months of growing before they produce their first harvest in the winter months. Turnips are nutrient-rich root crops that are delicious in soups and salads.

Winter

What to Plant:

1. Brussels sprouts

Plant your Brussels sprouts during the winter months to grow throughout the entire season but harvest them when they are small to avoid the worst of the harsh weather conditions from damaging them. Brussels sprouts are grown best indoors or in greenhouses where you can keep the temperature constant. Harvest small sprouts when they grow beyond small leaves and leave them in your garden for a second harvest during late spring and summer.

2. Parsnips

Parsnips are roots that require a lot of nutrients and water to survive, so if you have limited resources for growing food crops, this might not be the crop for you. Parsnips can be planted in planting holes that are a little on the small side because they grow best when they have room to spread out. Plant parsnips in fall and then again during the winter months when temperatures are below freezing but harvest them when they grow beyond small leaves, or else you will damage them.

3. Carrots

Carrots grow well throughout the winter months if there is enough warmth to start their growth process without the need for a lot of water and nutrients. Plant your carrots in the fall to give them enough time to grow during the winter months but harvest them when they are no longer little seedlings. Carrots can be grown inside or outside, but they will not grow well in too warm seasons, like summertime or fall.

4. Rutabagas

Rutabagas are a root crop that requires cool temperatures to survive, but when planted in warm soil, it will cause them to turn bitter; therefore, if you plan to grow rutabagas, you need to plant them in early fall or late winter for a second harvest during the springtime. Rutabagas are great crops for those gardeners who want to grow food inside because they do well indoors and still produce roots when grown outside; however, they do not grow very large.

5. Shallots

Onions and garlic are related to shallots, but shallots are bulbous. Plant shallots in fall and again during the winter months to give them enough time to grow during the winter months but harvest them when they are still small bulbs. Shallots can be grown outside or inside, but the temperature needs to be between 50- and 75-degrees Fahrenheit to produce well.

6. Chives

Plant chives in fall and again during the winter months for a second harvest. Chives are related to onions and garlic, but they are grown as green staples for flavoring foods and medicinal purposes. Chives can be grown indoors or outdoors, but they grow best in cool temperatures between 45- and 60-degrees Fahrenheit.

7. Horseradish

Horseradish is a root crop that grows best when planted in fall, but it can also be replanted during the colder months of winter if you live in an area that is not too warm or cold. Horseradish roots are eaten grated or sliced into soups, salads, and other cooked dishes to add a flavorful kick to any meal. Horseradish can be grown outdoors or in a greenhouse, but it will not grow well in too warm areas.

8. Kohlrabi

Kohlrabi is a root crop that produces a vegetable-like bulb; however, it still needs time to grow before you harvest it, so plant kohlrabi in mid-fall for the winter months to grow all season long. Kohlrabi is related to cabbage and is good for those gardeners who prefer a dense food crop because it produces many roots without much effort.

9. Broccoli

Broccoli is another very easy vegetable to grow; however, this time of year will be the ideal time to plant your broccoli because of the cool weather and because most of your other crops will have already been harvested by now. Broccoli grows best when planted in fall and then again in early winter so that it can give you a second harvest all season long. Broccoli can be grown indoors or outdoors, but it does not grow well in too warm areas during the summer months.

10. Celery

Celery will grow from the beginning of fall until mid-winter, but it can also be planted in late winter after you have harvested your other crops. Celery is used for flavoring foods and medicinal purposes because it contains high amounts of vitamins and minerals to rejuvenate the body. Celery needs very little water or nutrients to survive. You can plant celery in pots or directly in the ground but avoid planting it in areas that are too warm or too cold because celery does not respond well to extreme conditions.

The vegetables mentioned above are ideal for gardeners who plant within their own space and do not have a lot of resources to grow a lot of food crops. Planting in certain seasons will determine when you can harvest, but if you cannot plant during the listed times, that does not mean your crops will be unproductive. Depending on your area, you can plant your crops year-round, but be aware that your harvest times will be different, and the crops' speed will vary. Winter is when most gardeners begin to think about planting new seeds, although summer is ideal for those who want to continue to grow even after the other seasons have passed.

Gardeners who plant more than two crops can also benefit from planting their crops at times when the weather is no longer very hot or cold and everything is still growing well. Some gardeners decide to change their planting times depending on the location of their gardens because one climate may not be ideal for every type of vegetable.

Remember to plant your food crops in beds that are not overly prepared to save more resources to benefit your garden. Practice planting and harvesting from your garden at least once per season to become familiar with its resources and how they can best be managed.

CHAPTER 5: WATER SYSTEMS TO DESIGN FOR GARDEN

Most plants require regular watering to survive, and even the most drought-tolerant will require a drink occasionally. Numerous factors contribute to determining the optimal way to meet your garden's water requirements. Creating a robust water system for your garden is an important part of maintaining its health, and a correctly designed system will take care of some of the water needs of most plants.

In addition to the temporary watering that you occasionally do, your plants need an adequate and reliable water supply available throughout the season. Your garden should be able to provide enough water during dry periods in a way that will not cause any unnecessary damage to the environment or harm people and animals.

You want to design your garden's water system to offer enough water for your plants on its own without requiring you to monitor or adjust things constantly.

Things to Consider When Designing Your Garden's Water System

You want to design your garden's water system to offer enough water for your plants on their own without requiring you to monitor or adjust things constantly.

1. How Much Water Is Enough?

The quantity of water required each time can depend on several factors, including soil type and climate. Your plants' water requirements are determined by their size, type, and the environment in which they grow.

If you grow a vegetable garden, you will want to provide enough water for your plant roots to grow, but not overwatered. Depending on the type of plant you're trying to grow, you'll need varying amounts of water. Still, most vegetables require plentiful water with some supplemental irrigation during dry periods. Still, if you have many plants, your system might need to supply more than what one can do or supply in a day.

2. The climate

You should know how much water your plants will need to stay healthy during periods when no water is added to your system, such as during winter. If you live in a region with enough rain, you do not need to design a system that supplies more than the amount of rain you would normally get.

Proper water management is key when planning any garden; extremely dry or wet conditions can cause severe damage. You will want to be prepared and adequately equipped to deal with these fluctuations.

3. Types of plants you're growing

If you are growing mainly vegetables, then a smaller water intake will be needed than if you cultivated rare breeds of herbs and flowers that have a very strong need for water, such as cactus. For example, a vegetable garden usually requires less water than a cactus garden.

4. Where your system is located

Your location will play a large role in determining how much water each plant needs; for example, the amount of rain and humidity required for a tropical plant will be significantly less than an arid desert plant.

You want to ensure that your system provides enough water for your plants yet not become a potential flood hazard. You will want to consider how much water your system can provide and how easy it would be for you to defend against any rise in water. You might need to decrease or increase the amount of water being supplied at certain times depending on the weather conditions and different plant requirements.

5. How quickly do you want to see results with your garden

You can design your water system to provide enough water for your plants on its own, and you never need to supply additional watering. You might want to provide a substantial amount of the plant's water needs with the system itself but supplement the system with additional water each time you rinse- this way, you can make sure that everything is watered adequately but still give your garden some extra care. If your garden is large or contains a lot of plants that require a lot of water, you should think about how easy it will be to maintain and care for it.

6. Ease of use and maintenance

It is crucial that your system can be maintained and operated easily, especially if you have a large garden with many plants. You need to be able to check on your garden frequently, and water it to make sure that everything is functioning correctly, and the system is doing what you want it to do.

7. How large the garden is

The amount of water a system can provide and how much you need to provide for each plant depends on the size of your garden. If you have a small garden, it will be much easier for you to check on your plants and add water yourself. For example, if you can only measure 1" of soil moisture each day, then a very precise amount of water would be needed. A large garden can require more water depending on which plants are larger and their need for nourishment.

8. Whether the garden is new or old

Suppose your garden has previously been planted, and you add new plants. In that case, you'll want to think about whether you already have a system in place that includes a watering system and can simply be extended to provide enough water for the entire garden—or whether the new plants have very different needs. It can be extremely important to add additional water as needed throughout the season so that your plants do not become weak and unhealthy.

9. Need for irrigation other than simply watering

Different times of the year demand different types of water management. When planning your garden's water system, you will want to ensure that your system can provide enough water even if there are dry periods, or you might need to add more water at other times of the year. It would help if you considered what your garden needs for different seasons and how much water would be needed each time you add water to your system. Ensure that you can provide enough water for your plants when they need it most, such as during dry spells or a period of drought.

10. Other factors

No matter how well you plan and design your irrigation system, other factors might affect the system's performance. You might have to adjust the system or even repair it as needed because of weather conditions or any other unforeseen circumstances that might crop up.

You should consider the amount of evaporation when using your system to know how much water is being used. Some people do not include evaporation when deciding how much water should be in the system, but they will often be disappointed with the results. The evaporation rate can vary depending on various factors, such as how often you turn on your system and how efficient it is. Other factors that influence how quickly your water evaporates, such as wind and temperature, should be considered as well.

When deciding on how much water you will need, you should consider how much water is available to your plants at a given point in time. For example, if your system does not have enough water to meet the needs of your plants (for example, during a drought), you can add more water until the plants are rehydrated and healthy again. If there is too much water in an area, you can lower the amount being supplied by removing hose sections from your irrigation system.

To be certain that you can meet the watering needs of your garden, you should consider all these factors when deciding how much water your system will need.

CHAPTER 6: TYPES OF WATER SYSTEMS FOR YOUR GARDEN

The water supply should depend on your budget, the plants you are growing, the amount of time for which you want to maintain your garden, and the type of water pressure your garden has.

There are three main water systems for your garden: pressure-fed, gravity-fed, and drip irrigation.

Pressure-Fed Water Systems

Pressure-fed means that a pressurized water system is being used to supply water to the plants. These systems usually have a main hose leading from the water source to the end of the garden and then have lines that branch off into smaller hoses. These smaller hoses are laid out in rows throughout the garden and are connected by emitters or sprayers to each plant. One emitter or sprayer per plant will be buried under the soil next to each plant's base.

Advantages of Pressure-Fed Water Systems

1. Can supply water to large gardens with ease

Pressure-fed systems can easily supply water to large gardens and provide enough water for a larger garden with very few plants. The main advantage of this type of system is that it is simple to install and maintain, as you don't need much in the way of a pump or other plumbing. These systems can also be used in areas where there might be standing pools or lakes, so you won't have to worry about moving the source of your water source if an area changes suddenly.

2. Supplies adequate water quickly in most cases

In most cases, pressure-fed systems can provide enough water fairly quickly, within five minutes after they have been turned on. This is much faster than other watering systems, which usually take a few hours to several days to fill. This type of system can supply water quickly because it uses pressurized water, which can force water through the lines faster than gravity-fed systems.

3. No flooding or runoff

The main advantage of pressure-fed systems compared to gravity-fed or drip irrigation is that you don't have to worry about flooding or runoff as you water your garden. However, if you have a large garden and there might be some rain or flooding, you should consider adding more water to your system in advance to be ready to handle the water when it does come.

4. Easy to install

Pressure-fed systems are very easy to install. Simply run a hose from a faucet or another water source to your garden, laying down lines and plant emitters for each plant as you go. The hoses must be placed evenly throughout the garden so that no plants will be left out of the range of water. You can also use this type of system if you have multiple levels in your garden, such as raised beds with different depths of dirt. Just make sure that the emitters are placed where they will still be able to supply water to all layers.

5. Can be used in gardens that are not connected to a water main

Some homes or buildings might not have the water main running directly to your garden, so if you are going to use a pressure-fed system, you should check first to see if there is another way of supplying water, such as by using a well or an underground pipe. If you do have access to an existing water source, you can use this type of system instead because it uses only gravity. Unlike other watering systems, pressure-fed systems do not need power and don't need pumps other than the one at the water source.

6. Can be used in areas where there is a high-water table

If you have an area with a high-water table, such as flood plains or bogs, you can use pressure-fed systems because they do not risk clogging due to this higher water level. The main advantage of using pressure-fed systems for these areas is that your garden will receive a steady water supply, regardless of changes in weather conditions.

7. Can be used in areas that might have standing pools or lakes

Some areas with large water bodies, such as ponds and lakes, can also be used for pressure-fed systems. If you are sure that it is safe to do so, you can use this system to supply water to your garden. However, you'll need a different solution for each body of water, and you'll need to make sure the hoses for each one can handle the volume of any runoff or flooding from the body of water.

8. Easier to keep clean up time

If you have a large garden and need to clean up debris frequently, pressure-fed systems are easier than other types because they require fewer hoses, emitters, and overall parts to maintain. You won't have to be concerned about pipe leaks or difficult-to-replace parts, as you would with some other types of systems.

9. Leaves no runoff

Because pressure-fed systems use pressurized water, there is no risk of flooding and no chance for runoff. This helps prevent erosion problems in your garden and your home and helps keep your groundwater clean enough to be used again without any major issues.

10. Can be used with any container

In gardens that use containers or planter boxes, there are some benefits and drawbacks to using pressure-fed systems. The main benefit is that you can use a variety of planter containers if the holes in the box are large enough to fit your emitters through. However, you will have to keep in mind that it will be harder to water every plant with every size and kind of container because water will have to come from all sides of the box or container. You can still adjust this problem by ensuring that each plant gets enough water when it is being watered.

Disadvantages of Pressure-Fed Water Systems

1. It is not easy to install and maintain

This water system is not easy to install and maintain, especially using a good pump or other diverters. You need to ensure that the lines are laid out properly, but you also need to monitor them daily because the system will stop working when there is any damage or clogging. Each line must be checked for damage regularly and treated if necessary (by repairing it first and then adding fresh water). It can also be difficult to repair these systems quickly in the event of any problems because your water source might not always be nearby.

2. Hoses often get clogged because they are underground

One of the most common drawbacks of pressure-fed systems is that hoses often become clogged because they are buried underground or under mulch or other materials that can block small spaces in the line. To maintain your system properly, it will be necessary to check each hose inch regularly and make sure that the emitters are working properly. You may also want to consider adding an anti-clogging agent, such as bio-degradable detergents or fertilizer, as these can help prevent clogging in your hoses and lines for a short time.

3. Water might not reach all plants in a garden

The biggest drawback of pressure-fed systems is that they can be unevenly distributed. Some plants might get more water than others, or some may not receive any water because of clogging issues, blockages, or lack of emitters for that plant. This can result in poor growth or even death of some of your plants. You may need to do additional research on plants that are particularly sensitive to water levels, such as those intended for the desert or other arid conditions with very low water tables.

4. Sometimes can cause root rot and other problems

Another drawback of pressure-fed systems is that they can sometimes cause root rot or other damage to the plants, especially if the soil becomes waterlogged. This situation would be more common if your garden has a high-water table since the roots will become encased in water-logged mud or clay, making them susceptible to root rot. If you do not want to risk this happening, then you should consider using a drip irrigation system instead of a system where you are simply pumping the water into your garden with a hosepipe.

5. Cannot be used in areas where there is an active fire hazard

You should not use pressure-fed systems in areas with a high risk of fires (such as near a forest), as the water from these can easily cause fires. Similarly, if you are using it in a greenhouse or any area where there is a possibility of anything flammable catching fire, you should choose an alternate type of system.

6. It can be difficult to clean up if there is a lot of debris

Using a pressure-fed system, you will have more work to do after every rainstorm because it might be easy for leaves, mulch, or other debris to clog the lines. Under all circumstances, you should clear the hoses and emitters off your soil as soon as possible so that nothing gets lodged in them, and make sure that the hoses are not stretched or twisted at any point. This will improve the delivery of water and prevent clogs.

7. May have to use more water than other types of irrigation systems

Some people prefer a pressure-fed system because it allows them to use the same amount of water for their entire garden, which means less time and resources used for the water. However, more water may be wasted from a larger hose pipe and might make the garden susceptible to overwatering problems.

8. It might cause more algae growth than other types of systems

If your garden is prone to algae growth problems, you should consider using a drip irrigation system instead of a pressure-fed system. With a drip irrigation system, there will be little chance of algae getting clogged up in the hoses or around the emitters and causing an issue.

9. Requires more maintenance and care than other systems

Although a pressure-fed system can be more efficient, it requires more maintenance and care than other systems. You will have to check the water lines regularly and ensure that the emitters are working. You will also have to keep your water source clean, so you must regularly inspect your well or any other type of water source you are using. If there is even a slight problem with your water source, then your entire system could become contaminated so that it becomes useless.

10. May require more techniques for delivery than drip irrigation systems

The main advantage of drip irrigation systems is that they use less water but still deliver it directly to the roots of the plants via small holes. Some people prefer these systems because they allow them to deliver as little water as possible while still ensuring that the plants receive it. However, pressure-fed systems have a more difficult time reaching the roots of all your plants – especially if you have dense trees or other large plants in your garden – and might require some additional techniques to ensure that it delivers water properly to all your plants.

Types of Pressure-fed irrigation systems

There are several different types of pressure-fed irrigation systems available for purchase, including those mounted on posts above the ground, those with above-ground tanks, and those buried underground, but you can adjust them. The main differences between these systems are how they deliver the water and how easy it is to clean up the water delivery lines after a heavy rainstorm.

1. Mounted on posts

The most common type of pressure-fed system is mounted on posts, which will deliver the water directly underneath your plants. This type is more commonly used in gardens where there are trees or large plants installed above ground, but they can also be buried underground and still protected from the ground by bricks or pavers, depending on where you live.

2. Above ground tanks

Some pressure-fed systems are designed to work with a large container that holds the water for your garden. The water is delivered into the tank, and then you will have to go out every time you want to give your plants more water. These systems are more commonly used with gardens that have small areas of land, such as terraced gardens or little trees and shrubs, but can also be used in larger gardens if they have enough water stored in their tanks. Because of the need to empty the system upon every use, these might not be ideal for areas where you do not want to use up all your water at one time, such as a reservoir.

3. Buried systems

These systems work by burying the delivery lines and the emitters underground, but you can still install them on posts or above-ground tanks. These are considered less vulnerable to clogging, which makes it easier to clean up after heavy rainstorms, but they can still be prone to other problems in areas with a lot of debris.

4. Deep-soil systems

These systems are like buried systems and work in the same way, except that they can go even deeper into the soil, making them more effective for delivering water to your plants. However, these systems can require a lot of work because you will have to dig deep holes for each delivery line or all at once if you dig one big hole. In addition, these types of systems may take longer for the water to get delivered because it must travel a longer distance once it is in the soil.

5. Water-wheel systems

A water wheel system is a pressure-fed system that works by using energy from a moving stream of water to turn a wheel, which will then turn the lines and allow them to deliver water. These systems can be expensive and require working streams, but they can deliver a lot of water if you have a well or other fresh source close to your garden.

Choosing the best Pressure-fed system for your sustainable garden

Because of all the different types of pressure-fed systems available, it may not be easy to know which one is the best for you and your garden. The most important factors that you will have to consider are the size of your garden, whether you need to use a lot of water, and any other plants or trees in your garden that need water.

1. Consider your size

When determining which type of pressure-fed system is the best for you, there are some things that you should consider first, such as whether your garden is small. Like with other types of irrigation systems, larger gardens tend to require more water than small gardens do, so you will need to decide where you will put your system and how much water you will have to use in your garden if a large amount of it is needed.

2. Think about water requirements

To figure out how much water you will need each year with your chosen type of pressure-fed system, add up the total amount of inches that all the plants in your garden can use daily and then multiply that number by 3, 4, or 5, depending on how many times per day your plants want their water. Then round down your total number to the nearest inch, multiply that number by 3, 4, or 5 and then add 20% to it depending on whether you live in a high-humidity area. For example, if you have a garden with 9 plants that need an inch of water per day, you will multiply 9 inches by 3 to get 27 inches and then round down this number to 24 inches. You could then multiply your total number by 4 (24 x 4 = 96) and then add 20% to your total amount of water for the day (96 + 20 = 116).

3. Consider large trees or other plants

If you have large trees or tall shrubs, or other plants in your garden, those will take up a lot of space and might require more water than your smaller ones, so consider this when getting your pressure-fed system. The size of your system will also depend on how many plants you have in your garden, so if you want a lot of water available for all of them, get a system that will be able to deliver at least 250 gallons per hour.

4. Consider the weather and when you will use the water

Consider where you live or plan to install your pressure-fed system before deciding to buy one. If you live in an area with heavy rainstorms and need to clean up after them, then make sure that your system will be able to handle this job and prevent any clogs.

5. Consider the environmental impact

Let's say you're concerned about the impact of a pressure-fed system on the environment. In that case, you should make sure that it is less harmful compared to other irrigation systems and avoid using any chemicals or toxins in your soil. Also, remember only to use water that has been treated with a water purification system.

Starting Your Pressure-fed system

If you plan to start your pressure-fed system, you will have to make sure that you have the right raw materials, tools, and know-how to build your system. In addition, you should also consider what kind of site it is going to be placed on and if it will be underground or above ground for easy access.

1. Know how to build your system

While buying a prefabricated system with all the hard parts already assembled may seem appealing, building your own system will be much more efficient and streamlined. In addition, you will also have more freedom in designing your system, so make sure you pick a compact system since it will have to be put together in a small space.

2. Pick the right site for your system

Before you install your system, you will have to decide where you want it to go and make sure that it is possible to bury the pipes. If you want your system to be above ground, then pick a place where they will be safe from animals and humans that might interfere with them. Once you decide on a place, mark out the dimensions of where you want your system to go and cut out any trees or other plants there. The area must be flat so there are no problems with uneven lines. Make sure you dig a hole big enough for all of your pipes leading up to your main water inlet pipe. In addition, make sure there is enough room for the existing system to be put in and for the people who will be installing it.

3. Pick the right materials for your system

Once you have decided where you will install your system and what pipes you will need, you will have to decide which materials you want to use in your system. Although most are easy and cheap, certain materials can be toxic.

Materials:

- Polybutylene pipe: is used in pressure-fed systems because it is very durable and resilient. Also, it won't freeze as easily as copper or other metals might. In addition, you will have to open the pipes at least once a year to change the tubes around, so this can end up costing you more money than using other material types.
- Fiberglass pipe: is also a good type of material to use in your pressure-fed system because of its durability; it is lightweight, can handle higher temperatures, and is resistant to many chemicals. However, because it must be soldered together, it is more difficult to install than other types of material.
- Vinyl or PVC pipe: this pipe has been used for years in pressure-fed systems because it doesn't break as

easily, can work well in extreme heat and doesn't corrode as copper does.

4. Get the right tools for your system

Since you have to put a lot of people's hours into building any system and because making mistakes can be dangerous, you have to pick the right tools to do the job properly. It would help if you also got the most durable ones available for your specific job since this will save money in the long run and help reduce injuries and blemishes in your work.

Some of these tools include:

- Shovel
- Hoe
- Gloves
- Saws
- Tongs
- Drill
- Wrenches
- Hammers and Nails

How to install a pressure-fed system

If you are interested in installing your system, you must know how to do this safely without hurting yourself or damaging the pipes. For example, it's not recommended to dig up the pipes and layout the water pipes on their side since this can put pressure on the line, which could cause damage. Instead, make sure that they are level with one another and where things should be installed before you get to work.

Step 1: Make sure the prepared area is flat and ready to be used.

Step 2: Dig a hole big enough for all your pipes leading up to your water inlet pipe. In addition, make sure there is enough room for the existing system to be put in and for those who will install it.

Step 3: Install your main water line from where it comes into the house or out of a well until it hits the main water line outside of your house or at least two feet away. Ensure the pipe has no leaks or breaks before proceeding with any other steps.

Step 4: Install your main water line from where it leaves the main water pipe outside your house or at least two feet away.

Step 5: Dig a hole next to where you placed your inlet pipe that is big enough for the drainage pipe, and make sure there is a hole in the middle of it so that any excess water can drain out.

Step 6: Add the extra piping to your main system inside the house and connect it to the main lines to test it properly. Before filling any holes with dirt, rocks, or other materials you've purchased, double-check that all your lines are straight and down with no kinks or bends.

Step 7: Go out to the main water line and make sure it is not leaking before using tarps to cover it up so it doesn't get any leaks while installing your system.

Step 8: Now that everything looks straight, and down with no leaks, you can go back inside the house and install your additional piping where it goes into your house.

Before applying any pressure to the lines, you may need to install air filters in some cases. Make sure the pipes have proper ventilation since they could be too hot if there are too many people working with them or if they are not ventilated sufficiently enough.

Installing a system or redoing the one already set up can be time-consuming. Hence, many people hire professionals to install these systems, saving themselves the stress and time of   figuring out things on their own. However, it is important to plan everything out before hiring anyone and ensure the person you hire has done this before. Although an experienced professional can charge more than someone new, he will be able to do the job more efficiently, so you won't have to do it yourself and pay twice as much for his work.

CHAPTER 6.1: DRIP IRRIGATION SYSTEM

A drip irrigation system might be good for new gardeners with small garden spaces who wish to reduce garden maintenance. The system has a main hose leading away from the water source that runs along the length of your garden. Sprayers or drippers are then connected by smaller hoses to each plant, with one per plant. You can adjust the amount of water supplied to each plant by moving the emitters further or closer to it. This will provide more or less water as your plants go through the different stages of growth.

Advantages of Drip Irrigation System

1. Provides more precise watering

With drip irrigation, you can control how much water any plant receives and for how long. This increases your chances of avoiding over-or under-watering your plants, both of which can cause problems in your garden. The drip system also allows you to choose exactly when each plant gets watered, so you can water it at night if that is what you prefer.

2. Less maintenance

Compared with other watering systems, drip irrigation requires less attention and less time for maintenance during the summer months, which gives new gardeners a chance to focus on other parts of their garden or other projects. If you have the right timer for your system, you can set it and forget about it.

3. Faster growth

Although drip irrigation requires you to do a bit of work initially, such as setting up the system and installing a timer, the advantage is that your plants will grow much faster because they are getting exactly what they need to grow. The irrigation system will also keep your garden looking nice throughout the season, reducing maintenance time.

4. Saves water and energy

Because drip irrigation systems only give each plant as much water as it needs at a given time, it saves both water and energy. This is especially important in areas where growing plants in the summer means using a lot of water and energy for air conditioning.

5. Reduces waste

Drip irrigation also reduces waste because the plants are getting what they need to grow. However, keep in mind that drip irrigation requires more work initially and consumes more electricity than other systems, which means your plants may still require additional fertilizer and care to grow optimally.

6. Adjustable water flow

Adjustable water flow is a positive feature of drip irrigation systems. The system can be adjusted to perform the task according to different crops' climatic conditions and moisture requirements by adjusting the water flow.

7. Reliable supply of nutrient-rich water

Unlike flood or overhead irrigation, drip irrigation ensures that each plant gets just enough nutrient-rich water to grow perfectly. This saves time and energy for farmers, who no longer need to spend long hours watering their fields manually. Drip irrigation also conserves water, which has become an important issue in many countries nowadays, ensuring no water waste in agricultural processes.

8. The system is durable

The water pressure is controlled and released at intervals, which ensures a constant flow of nutrient-rich water to the roots of plants. It also ensures that the soil doesn't become waterlogged and there is no runoff of water into drains or bodies of water, which can cause pollution. Unlike overhead irrigation systems, drip irrigation systems are easy to maintain and cost-effective.

9. Removable tubing

The flexible tubing used in drip irrigation systems is completely removable, making it much easier to clean and sterilize. The same flexibility also allows you to use the system in areas where it may be difficult to install uprights, such as under a deck or concrete wall. The removable tubing also provides for a more versatile installation of the system, which means that you can bend it to fit different spaces or crops.

10. Efficient dispersion of water

Drip irrigation ensures that water is continuously released from emitters into the soil with minimal loss, resulting in an efficient flow over and around each plant's root. This allows for a more even water distribution over the plants and increases efficiency.

Drip irrigation is a way to apply water by using low pressure to drip small amounts of water at regular intervals into the soil around the root zone of each plant. This can be done through tubing placed on or below ground level or even through the drippers that utilize containers to catch and hold water. The use of drip irrigation increases the efficiency with which water is used. A properly designed drip irrigation system can reduce fertilizer and pesticide use while maximizing yields per pest free area.

Disadvantages of Drip Irrigation

1. More expensive to install

While drip irrigation saves time and money in other parts of the garden, it can be more expensive to install compared to other water systems because you need a timer or other device to control the system. If you do not want to invest in a timer, your only option will be to water at predetermined times throughout the day, which will make your garden appear less natural and require additional maintenance time. Also, the setups of many drip irrigation systems can be too complicated to install.

2. Removable tubing reduces efficiency

The tubing is easily removed from the water emitters and can require replacement for various reasons, reducing the system's efficiency in these cases.

3. Not appropriate for all climates

Drip irrigation is most effective in areas with little rainfall because it reduces the amount of water required to grow plants. It also works well in areas where the summers are expected to be warm and dry because drip irrigation can be used to supplement natural irrigation by drawing water from deeper ground levels to provide summer watering. It is not a good option for cold weather climates or frequent rain areas because it can easily clog up with mud and dirt.

4. Drip irrigation systems are not compatible with all plants or with all soil types

Some trees and ornamental plants will not grow well on drip irrigation because their root structures do not fit into the system well enough or because they have roots that will rot from being exposed too long to water in this manner. Some plants will also require more water than the emitter can provide. If you are using drip irrigation with trees, you must install a valve pre-filter on the line between the tree and the drip line. This filter must be replaced regularly because it clogs easily. It is also critical to keep your emitter lines clear of organic matter and blockages, which can cut off their supply of nutrients and water.

5. Pest Control

Drip irrigation may require more pest control in some cases. In areas with many mosquitoes, these pests will be attracted to the structure that provides water and can become a problem. They do not attract moths and other pests to the structure, but you should still invest in insect control for your garden.

6. Fertilizer use may increase with drip irrigation

Just like plants need regular fertilizing, so do emitter systems. The emitter typically has a system built into it that facilitates the controlled release of water into the soil. In some cases, this system will require more frequent fertilization than other irrigation systems because it does not have the option to be turned on and off as often or to use chemicals or soluble fertilizers. This applies to dry soils, which require very little fertilizer but a great deal of water for optimal growth.

7. Not good for large gardens

Drip irrigation systems work best with smaller land areas and cannot handle larger operations easily. They are also not appropriate for commercial farming situations because they cannot handle large plots of land or numerous crops at one time.

8. It can be difficult to install in areas with hills or slopes

Drip systems only work well where there is not a lot of slope or difference in levels. If there are any differences in levels, rainfall can accumulate too much water in high spots and then flow straight down into low spots, wasting water and causing clogging on the emitter lines. Because it is difficult to install drip irrigation systems in areas with these problems, you may want to consider some other watering system for your garden.

9. Not good in areas with high winds

Because the emitters are installed on short lines, they can be damaged by high winds and heavy rains. Ensure that your emitters have proper protections, so they will not be damaged if the lines become tangled or if the water pressure is too strong for your system's design.

10. Difficult to install adjacent to pools

Drip irrigation systems are not recommended for use in areas directly adjacent to pools because the water pressure from the pool will damage the tubing. Additionally, some emitters use plastic which can be damaged by sunlight and heat from solar radiation. These emitters are not warrantied against damage and do not last long under these conditions.

Types of drip irrigation

1. In-line emitters

Drip tape or tubing is the most popular commercial drip irrigation system, and home gardeners use it. The watering emitter is installed at intervals along a water supply line, such as 1/4-inch tubing on nursery rows 5' apart. The tubing is placed vertically in the ground with plastic risers every 18", or horizontally if used on a roof reservoir that gravity feeds to each plant. Unless otherwise specified, a properly designed system will have emitters spaced no more than 30 feet apart. Drip tapes are often protected from wind damage using windsocks on plants such as tomatoes and pole beans.

2. Surface irrigators

Sometimes called a bubbler system, this system uses plastic tubing like drip irrigation. Plants are spaced further apart— compared to drip irrigation— usually about 3' apart in order to avoid clogging. . Plastic risers are used every 18" or so in the ground to keep the emitters from clogging with mud and debris. A bubbler comes on after 5 minutes of watering and then shuts off after the water has drained from the emitters. This system is often used for a very small area where a few plants need regular watering. It is not intended for larger areas such as rows of vegetables or fruit trees because the water pressure is insufficient to move the water through the tubing.

3. Vertical emitters

This system similarly uses vertical plastic tubing for drip irrigation, but it takes longer to deliver water through the tubing than with a drip irrigation system. The emitter is installed vertically on a distribution pipe at intervals of 30 feet (12') and spaced no more than

54 feet apart, which is almost dead center in a row of plants. The emitter comes on after five minutes and will shut off two hours after the lines were last watered. A nozzle must be installed at each end of the distribution pipe to dispense water at the end of the emitters. This system is often used for large areas such as rows of vegetables because it does not waste water running up and down the pipes.

4. Ground irrigation

This system is exactly like a bubbler system, except that it uses buried tubing instead of plastic risers. Plastic risers will clog with mud and debris more quickly when used in a ground situation, and they risk damage from high winds, particularly on uneven ground. To avoid clogging, emitters are spaced further apart than with an in-line emitter, and grown plants are spaced 3' apart in most cases. A bubbler comes on after 5 minutes of watering and then shuts off after the water has drained from the emitters. This method is often used for a very small area where a few plants need regular watering. Because the water pressure required to move the water through the tubing is insufficient, it is not suitable for larger areas such as rows of vegetables or fruit trees.

5. Universal irrigation

This system uses flow channels filled with water, so it is not an irrigation system. For example, the flow channels are placed above plants or under pots in gardens and watering zones on golf courses. Water passes through the channels through nozzles or openings located at each end of the flow channel. The combination of gravity and a high-water pressure causes the water to trickle through the channels while the emitter is on. After five minutes, the emitter will turn off when the water coming out of the nozzle or opening stops flowing.

6. Soaker hoses

Soaker hoses are made from many materials such as plastic or rubber, and even recycled materials like old tires. The soaker hose is placed into trenches next to planting beds and drips water along its entire length, up to 100 yards in some cases. There are also drip hoses for lawns that work similarly to these soaker hoses for gardens.

Starting Your Own Drip Irrigation System for Your Garden

If you decide to install drip irrigation in your garden, the following steps will show you how to set up a drip irrigation system for your garden.

1. Select the drip irrigation system that is right for you.

There are several distinct types available, each with its own set of advantages and disadvantages. The first thing you should consider is the size of your garden and the number of plants that will be using it. The next thing you should consider is what types of plants you will be growing. Then you need to determine if you have an adequate water source, if you have a sufficient water supply, and lastly, how long it will take before the water runs out.

2. Find the area where you will install the drip irrigation system.

Remember that because these irrigation systems need water pressure, you may need to dig trenches or make holes in sidewalks or driveways before installing these systems. Additionally, you may need to make room for electric wires or tubing if the system is powered by electricity.

3. Decide which type of irrigation system to use in your garden.

Not all of them are suitable for your garden, and not all work equally well in all situations. Some water emitters can get clogged with leaves and mulch and may not be suitable for use in a wild environment. Some emitters may not be suitable for use on a roof garden because the water pressure is insufficient to move water through the tubing.

4. Measure the distance between your plants and the drip line in your garden.

This step is important because a drip irrigation system has a preset water flow rate, and if the distance between plants is too small, it will not be able to supply enough water for all of them. The simplest method is to run a measuring tape along the inside of each row of plants from end to end.

How to install your Drip Irrigation System

Tools

- Tape measure
- Hammer
- Utility knife.

Materials Needed

- PVC Embellishments (pipes, caps, and risers)
- Good quality drip tape
- Fittings (garden hose fittings and sprinkler adapters)
- Water source (faucet,/ under-garden hose/ water tank/ etc.)
- Check valve (if needed)

Construction

Step 1: Prepare the Garden

Dig a trench around the garden that is wide enough for the drip irrigation system.

Ensure you have enough room for four or five rows of plants; it may not be necessary for every row to be completely piped, but this will depend on how big your garden is and how many plants you will be growing.

Step 2: Set the Water Source in Place and Close on the Edging

Ensure you have enough water to supply more than three rows of plants and all the edging. If you don't have enough water and there is a substantial gap between your plants, you may need to pump water from your source and place it under the edge of your drip irrigation system by running it into a bucket and then back up again. You will have to have something that can stop the flow, or you may need to use a check valve.

Step 3: Install Faucets on Each End of Each Section

Run piping around each row of plants and make sure that each row has its faucet into which you can connect the water source. The placement of faucets will depend on how many rows of plants you are growing. If you have only one faucet per row, then it is best to place them towards the middle of the row, as closer to your plants and farther from your water source.

Step 4: Install the Water Source in Each Section

The water source could be a faucet, hose, or another supply method. Ensure that it is not leaking when turned on and has enough pressure to supply the drip irrigation line.

Step 5: Install the Drip Line in Each Section

Install drip tape around each row of plants and ensure a good seal for each line. Installing an EZ-Drip connector, which consists of a stainless-steel collar, a stainless-steel ferrule, a rubber washer, and an O-ring, is the simplest way to accomplish this. Ensure that the O-ring is facing the drip line, push the drip tape into place, insert the ferrule and then tighten down the nut.

Step 6: Place in Each Section

Install any fittings needed to make each line fit together properly. These include elbows, tees, and end caps. An elbow will allow you to have a 90-degree turn; a tee will give you options in which direction the water flows through your hose, and end caps are used when you want to make a straight run out of your hose.

Step 7: Check for Leaks in Each Section

Once the drip irrigation system is installed, you'll need to check for any leaks in each section and make any fixes necessary. This can be done by using a flashlight and searching for water at night or placing a cup under each faucet and checking on it after an hour or two. Ascertain that no water is leaking from the system and that there are no drips near your faucets, as these could cause damage to your plants. If you find leaks, then fix them before continuing with the next step.

Step 8: Install the Drip Tape in Each Section

To make the dripping more efficient, there are two different ways to install the tape. One way is to completely cover each line with as much tape as possible, but this may cause extra pressure on your drip lines, so leaving a five or six-inch gap around each line is best. The other way is to use a splash guard and cover only half of each line. This allows you to use less tape and have less pressure on your drip lines or use more tape and have more pressure while keeping a small gap between your water sources and your drip lines. These options vary according to the type of plants you are growing and your personal preferences; therefore, consider which method is best for you.

Step 9: Test Your System

After your drip irrigation system is installed, it is important to ensure that everything works as it should. You'll need to check that there are no leaks in your lines or fittings and make any necessary fixes, then turn on each faucet and look for leaks or drips near them. Look at each tape and ensure that the water has reached all of them. Finally, check on how much water is being applied to each plant through your drip tape, as this may need to be adjusted depending on the type of plants you have.

Every Drip irrigation system will need different materials and constructions, and the example from above may differ depending on your personal preference or the conditions in your garden. The main idea is to ensure that all the materials are of good quality and that everything has been installed properly.

Each Drip irrigation system will have its own set of rules and regulations for when to be used, so make sure you familiarize yourself with these before you begin installing your irrigation system. This way, you'll earn your neighbors' trust and be able to develop a strong relationship that benefits everyone in your community.

Employing a professional may also help when it comes to installing the system. By using a professional, you will have someone more experienced with designing and installing Drip irrigation systems, so the job may seem easier in their hands.

If you want to use a drip line for houseplants, then several factors need to be considered. First and foremost, always test a small piece of your plant before putting it into your garden or home. This is especially critical if you have a particularly delicate plant, as it may break much sooner and more easily than you believe. Secondly, know the best location to site your drip lines—adding them to the bottom of your houseplants might cause damage that is difficult to repair and end up taking much longer than necessary.

Also, ensure that there are enough outlets for all your plants and that each plastic pipe has a proper fitting at each end. Check the tape to ensure that it is the right type for your plant and that it is firmly attached to the plastic pipe. Finally, make sure that there are no leaks around any of the connections in your drip irrigation system, as this could cause damage to your plants or even harm you or someone else.

CHAPTER 6.2: GRAVITY-FED WATER SYSTEMS

Gravity-fed systems rely on gravity to move water throughout your garden. The main hose is usually connected to the water source that holds backwater in a reservoir. Some hoses branch off the main hose and connect each emitter or sprayer with a plant, but these hoses are essentially gravity fed, as once they are attached to a plant, you will not need to maintain them. These systems can be very simple but require no maintenance at all.

Advantages of Gravity-Fed Water Systems

1. No initial installation costs

Gravity-fed water systems do not require an initial cost. If you already have a water source and a hose, gravity systems are extremely low cost. Gravity-fed systems generally have a much lower initial investment than other water systems.

2. No ongoing costs

The system requires no additional maintenance after installation, making it extremely low maintenance compared to drip irrigation or sprinkler systems. You can even add new plants without adding additional hoses or other devices to your system. This is especially handy for gardeners who only have a small amount of space for growing but want to add more plants later without installing anything else from scratch.

3. It is extremely low maintenance

You are not responsible for any plumbing or electrical system installation or maintenance. Your only job is to ensure your water source has enough water to work with, which can typically be taken care of through regular watering. You will also need some skills to install the system, but anyone with the proper knowledge can learn this skill quickly.

4. It is a flexible system

Gravity-fed systems are very flexible because they do not require more than one main hose. They can easily be adapted to any garden or yard and can even use various water sources. You could use a pond, creek, or running stream if your garden is near these sources. This saves you from having an entirely separate water supply for your garden.

5. It is low maintenance for the plants

Unlike other irrigation systems, gravity-fed systems are extremely low maintenance for the plants. They work with your plants by distributing water over them and do not require any additional chemicals or high pressure. You can even remove the hose from a plant and leave it in the ground to allow for roots to continue growing, providing you with a much lusher plant.

6. High yields per area of use

Gravity-fed systems are very efficient regarding how much water they can apply to a garden area. We can apply up to three times more water using gravity systems than drip irrigation, which means that crops can be fed more efficiently with gravity systems.

7. It is compatible with other water sources

Gravity-fed systems are also compatible with other water sources. They can be used with things like natural bodies of water and ponds, or they can be used with a simple faucet or hose at a nearby water source. This allows you to receive more water in your garden by utilizing the same system that delivers water to your yard. Alternatively, you could even use gravity systems for both watering and fertilizer watering, letting them handle the watering of your plants without troubling yourself too much about it being wasteful or cost-efficient.

8. There is no need for soil pipes or emitters

Gravity-fed systems do not require the use of soil pipes or emitters. Water flows directly from your water source to your garden. Because of this, gravity-fed systems are very fine in terms of how close plants can be to one another and will not clog up with roots and leaves.

9. It is very easy to install

Gravity-fed water systems are extremely easy to install. They do not require any pump or pressurized tubing, and they can be started similarly to a garden hose. You connect your water source to your hose and then place the hose where you would like water applied. This can be used for something as simple as watering a small number of plants in your yard, or it could be used for an entire vegetable garden that requires an entire watering system.

10. It is compatible with other container gardening styles

Gravity-fed water systems are compatible with other container gardening styles like vertical, indoor, and hydroponics. They can be used to irrigate the entire garden from one main supply of water, which is extremely convenient for container gardening.

Gravity-fed systems are also compatible with other container gardening styles like vertical, indoor, and hydroponics.

Disadvantages of Gravity-Fed Water Systems

1. It is not easy to modify existing systems

While it is easy to create a new gravity-fed water system from scratch, it is not easy to modify an existing watering system. If you need a new change in your garden or yard, you will need to install an entirely new system rather than make changes.

2. It is not a very efficient way to water plants

While gravity systems are efficient in terms of delivering water, they are not all that great at doing so when you compare them to other watering styles. The limited amount of water pumped through them means there can be dry spots in your yard even if the system is working properly.

3. It requires a substantial upfront cost to install

Gravity-fed systems require quite a bit of expense to install the water system from scratch, and the costs may vary depending on where you live and your specific needs. While this cost may be worth it, especially to people who have a large amount of land and various needs, it can be prohibitively expensive for smaller gardens.

4. It is not very efficient if the water source is already being used by someone else

Gravity systems are not very efficient compared to drip irrigation or drip systems. They can be used to water a relatively small area, and they are quite fine with nutrient-rich groundwater, but they cannot be used in places where people already use their water supply for another function. This means that you cannot use gravity-fed systems when using your water supply for other purposes, such as an available pond or stream nearby.

5. It requires labor-intensive maintenance to allow for easy removal of plants

Gravity systems do not allow you to remove the hose and leave it in the ground. It would be prudent to verify that the hose is not clogged, and that water is flowing freely throughout your system. Even if you are not actively watering your plants, you need to plan on always having a small bottle on hand. This can be slightly inconvenient most days but may mean that you will never have to remove the plants from your watering system, which can be convenient, especially if you want to fertilize or prune them instead of washing them or removing them from the system.

6. It is not the most efficient way to water a small number of plants

Gravity systems are not ideal for small gardens or small numbers of plants. They do not allow for the water to be distributed quickly enough to be used on a timely basis, and this means that you will have to go through your watering cycle several times with smaller gardens.

7. It does not work in terrains where gravity is often against you

Gravity-fed water systems work best in places with an existing body of water or stream nearby. They do not work well in places where gravity may be working against you, so they are difficult to apply if only a few sources are nearby.

8. The system is not very efficient, and it can clog up easily and become difficult to manage

Gravity-fed water systems do not have a high flow rate, meaning that they are quite fine for fertilizer water but are difficult to use for plant watering. They also tend to become clogged up about a week after installation or when used for fertilizer, which means that you need to check the pressure frequently and remove any leaves or debris from the system regularly. Adding new leaves that fall from plants in your yard can also cause problems with obstruction of your system unless you have access to another source of water nearby that you can use to clear the system.

9. It is not the best choice for large gardens or for gardens that require a lot of water

Gravity systems are not ideal for larger gardens and gardens that would require a lot of water to get through. They are great if you have small needs, but if your garden requires more than a drop, it's better to move away from gravity systems and look at other watering options like sprinklers or drip irrigation.

10. It is not the best choice for gardens that require an ongoing water source

This system is incompatible with gardens that require a constant water source in the ground, particularly if you have many plants that require regular watering. You should look at drip irrigation for your gardening needs, especially if your garden requires lots of water throughout the season.

Types of gravity-fed water systems for container gardening

1. Open top

Open top systems have no lid on the top, making them ideal for various plants. They can be used with full-sized containers as well as half-barrels and more. They are the easiest of all gravity-fed watering systems to set up, and they provide a convenient way to easily reach your plants while they are watering through the hose attached to your fixture.

2. Linkable

If your plants live in an area with no nearby water body, you can also use a linkable system. These systems require a high-pressure hose and an attached pump fueled by batteries or electricity for power. Pressure must be set at the pump, and the water comes through the loop created by the hose and down to the container, which means that there is less risk for blockages.

The downside of this is that if the pressure in the hose ever drops, the water supply will not flow through it, which is a real problem for gardens located in areas where water pressure is inconsistent.

3. Gravity barrel

Gravity barrel systems require a specific design and an "L" shaped hose with a steel ring around the top of the container to help create a closed system. The water flows downward through the hose and into the lower container, fitted with an overflow hole that allows you to easily add more water if necessary to keep your plants well-watered throughout their growth period. This system can be used in any number of containers and is easy to install. It also allows you to take up as much space as you need without worrying about exposing your plant to too much heat, cold, or light from the sun.

No matter how you look, gravity-fed watering systems are popular ways to water home and container gardens. They are easy to install, can be set up by anyone with the knowledge of following directions, and help maintain good health for your plants.

Starting Your Own Gravity-Fed Water System for Your Sustainable Garden

If you want to start your gravity-fed water system, there are a few things to be aware of.

1. Maintaining the system appropriately.

If you are using PVC piping, ensure that you maintain it properly to ensure that it does not clog up and make it difficult to use the water system later. There are a variety of products available to help you keep your piping flowing, but you may need to drain and restart if you run into any issues.

2. Finding an appropriate location for the water source.

Several places can be used as a water source for your gravity-fed watering system, including rain barrels and other water collection points in your yard like faucets and bathtubs. They are in an appropriate place and are functional enough to be used legitimately. Be sure that if you use your bathtub or another useful water source on your property, you maintain it appropriately to ensure that it remains convenient for future use.

3. Setting up the system properly to not clog up.

If you must restart your gravity-fed watering system because of an issue with a clogged-up pipe, consider using flexible tubing to ensure that there is no possibility of inadvertently blocking the flow of water into your garden. These tubes can help eliminate blockages and keep your garden watered properly but still allow the water to flow freely through them if the need arises.

4. Use a pump to move your water if necessary.

If you must move your water from one location to another, be sure that you invest in a pump that will help move the water during this time. If you do not use a pump, it will be difficult for your garden to receive enough water during dry periods and difficult for things such as plants with deep root systems or trees to get enough water without constant attention on your part when things become dry outside.

5. Over-watering is a concern to watch for.

Be sure that you do not over-water your plants, especially if you are using a gravity-fed watering system and would like to keep things simple for the plants in your area. If you are using a hose system with no flow control, it is possible to over-water your plants and cause them to die from over-watered roots eventually.

How to install a gravity fed water system
Materials

- PVC pipe - 1/2 to 1-inch diameter
- Dripline or hose - 1/2-to-3/4-inch diameter
- Stakes or strings for marking
- Tape measure, pencil, and marker

- Hacksaw, PVC pipe cutter, and connectors (or tubing cutter and a steady hand) NOTE: When cutting PVC pipe, wear safety glasses to protect your eyes.
- Screwdriver and hammer
- Drilling bits - 1/2-to-3/4-inch diameter
- Ganging bit - same as a screwdriver bit
- 5/32" drill bit - 1 inch
- 1" drill bit and drill
- Electrical tape (or hot glue)

Instructions

Step 1: Mark off your garden spacing.

Measure the distance between each container or spot and mark the points with a string, a big stick, or anything else that can be used to determine the distance between each plant. It would help if you considered using stakes or strings to remember where everything is about one another as you are doing your watering later in the season.

Step 2: Prepare the PVC pipe.

Using a hacksaw, cut the PVC pipes to length. You should use a PVC cutter or tubing cutter instead if you have one available to you. You mustn't cut straight across when cutting your pipe and end up with too short pieces because it can be difficult to connect some pieces if they are too small. Taking off a few extra inches from each pipe will ensure that this does not happen.

Step 3: Cut the drip line or hose.

Use the hacksaw or PVC cutter to cut the drip line or hose to length. You will want to cut these at least a foot longer than the longest length of your garden so that you can use the extra for any short pieces of pipe.

Step 4: Connect the tubing and pipe.

Take two hose connectors or two pieces of PVC pipe and connect them with a "T" connector or two slip couplings. This should allow you to connect the drip line or hose to both ends of your PVC pipe. You must make sure that nothing is kinked inside, which will cause blockages on either side and cause the system flow to be interrupted.

Step 5: Layout the tubing and pipe in your garden.

Use the tape measure to place the tubing and pipe straight in your garden. Keep it close to the walls as much as possible to allow for smooth flow of water which will not have a hard time navigating through your plants.

Step 6: Cut short pieces of tape and attach them to the pipes.

Use a hacksaw or PVC cutter to cut small pieces of tape for every four inches of pipe, starting at one end and working around both sides of the line. It would help if you were sure that these are long enough to lay flat on top of your garden when you are done with them later in the season and they do not get damaged or pulled off by anything too sharp during this period. You can get these pieces of tape at most hardware stores.

Step 7: Attach one side of the tape to the drip line or hose and the other side to the PVC pipe.

Attach some tape to the drip line or hose sides starting at one end and working your way around. This will ensure that it does not pull off during this process, and it also ensures that your lines do not kink anywhere inside.

Step 8: Attach all sides of both ends of the line, then put some weight on.

On both ends of the line, put some weight on to keep the line from unraveling. It would help if you were using stones or bricks for this to ensure that it does not pull off in an intense windstorm. Add enough weight to the tape so that it is level with the surrounding ground, without being too high or too low.

Step 9: Keep everything snug.

Once the tape is even with the ground around it, use a screwdriver and hammer to gently tap it down so that any peaks will be smoothed back out. You should also check for any points where you might have missed a spot in Step 4 and make sure that there are no holes or kinks in the line.

Step 10: Mark off your garden with a permanent marker.

After you've completed all of this, you should be able to start planting your garden. Mark, each end of the tubing or hose with permanent markers to tell which side is going into the water source and which one is for each section of your garden.

Frequently Asked Questions

Q: What materials can I use to connect my gravity-fed water system?

A: Much of the tubing used to install a drip irrigation system is flexible PVC, which allows it to bend and stay in one piece. You should avoid using metal in any heating, ventilation, and air conditioning (HVAC)system. When installing any tubing for gravity-fed water system, ensure that you do not use anything larger than 1/2" in diameter. When these pipes relate to typical couplings or slip-on connectors, they will cut into your hose or line if the pieces are too large. If you have small garden areas, this may not be an issue.

Q: Why does my watering system have to be pointed downwards?

A: The most common reason for this is simple physics. Gravity pulls down on everything, and when the water used for your drip irrigation system comes out of the pipe instead of just coming out at random angles, it will have greater force and spray a wider area. This will result in a much more efficient watering system in general, as well as a reduction in the likelihood of roots clogging your line over time.

Q: What kind of hose should I use for a gravity-fed water system?

A: There are many different hoses to choose from when setting up your gravity-fed water system on your personal property. It is important to research what sort of material is used in the hose you want to use, which will help with the longevity and flexibility of your hose over time.

Q: What are some good plants that I can grow using this watering system?

A: Many different plants can be grown using a gravity-fed water system, and there are many advantages to growing each one. You should consider how much water or sunlight different plants require, what type of soil they need, and whether they will attract pests if you grow them near your home. Some plants that grow well in gravity-fed water system include cucumbers, corn, carrots, lettuce, tomatoes, beans, and spinach.

Gravity-fed water system is more advanced and complex than some have thought before, but it doesn't have to be. Anyone can set it up for their garden with the right tools and knowledge, making life a little easier. The transition from traditional sprinkler systems to drip is not a tough one at all, and once you begin using your system, you will wonder how you ever lived without it.

CHAPTER 7: SEEDS

Seed management is the process of collecting and distributing seeds to the field.

Planting a sustainable garden is not just about the plants and the harvest. It's also about maintaining a sustainable supply of seeds for future planting.

Seed Saving

Seed saving is the process of gathering, storing, and distributing viable seeds from year to year. If you grow your seed, you are responsible for this process from start to finish. Seed saving can take time and effort beyond simply ordering seeds from the local garden center.

Ways to provide your garden with a sustainable seed supply

1. Save seed yourself

The first is to save seed yourself, and the second is to buy local, open-pollinated seed. When you save your seed, you control its origin and genetics—the plant traits that have evolved in response to the surrounding environment. Many of the advantages of local, open-pollinated seeds are lost if commercial hybrids are used. For example, if you plant a hybrid that has been bred to mature quickly, it is unlikely to spread by reseeding itself (which is one of the most sustainable ways that any plant species can reproduce).

Most commercial seed companies are part of a worldwide network that includes production facilities as far away as China and India. For example, many seed packets indicate their origin as Holland or Ontario. Even though these companies may be located relatively close to where you live, there is a great distance between them and whatever part of the world their seeds came from.

2. Buy local, open-pollinated seed

The second way to provide your garden with a sustainable seed supply is to buy open-pollinated seeds from local gardeners. Open-pollinated means that the seeds come from mother plants or other plants grown from the same original plant. When you grow open-pollinated seeds yourself, you are guaranteed genetic diversity from various mother plants growing in the same place and pollinating each other. The seeds will be more likely to reproduce themselves through reseeding rather than spreading by wind and water.

There are two types of open-pollinated seeds:

1. True open-pollinated seed

True open-pollinated seeds are seeds that have been grown from true open-pollinated plants. True open-pollinated plants are often hybrids or strains raised for specific traits but still produce viable seeds through sexual reproduction. This is often the case with common crops and vegetables such as tomatoes and peppers, which can be a mix of different genetic traits from multiple mother plants.

The true open-pollinated seed does not come from hybrid crosses. There is no mystery behind it, and it can be purchased from local gardeners or even online. True open-pollinated seed is often the most sustainable choice for breeding plants for traits such as fast growth. The seeds come from plant varieties that have been bred for characteristics but can still spread by seeding themselves in the surrounding environment.

2. Selected seed

Selected seed refers to a selected seed used to produce hybrid cultivars or new varieties of genetically modified plants. Many hybrids and genetically modified plants sold in nurseries, hardware stores, and garden centers come from selected seeds.

As discussed earlier in Chapter 1, this is not a sustainable type of seed. The genetic diversity is low compared to open-pollinated seeds, so if you save the seeds of a particular hybrid plant, they will most likely not be the same next year because they are not true open-pollinated seeds. Hybrids have another disadvantage: they often have lower germination rates than open-pollinated varieties of the same crop. Many hybrid seeds might produce viable new plants, but that group won't be very diverse either.

How to Determine if seed health is viable for planting
1. Check the seed packet for clues as to seed health.

If the seeds are viable, they should feel dry and brittle and not be soft or moist. Also, look for obvious damage, such as holes or tears in the packaging. Notice bruises on seeds, moldy or decaying seeds and separate from the rest of the group, ones that are bruised, shriveled, dry or hard to separate, and flattened seeds.

2. Seed vigor

Vigor refers to the health of a seed and its ability to sprout under proper growing conditions. A "vigorous" seed can germinate, grow, and produce a healthy plant within one season. The term does not refer to a plant's size or growth rate. Vigor indicates whether the seeds in the packet will be able to germinate and send roots into the soil within days of planting.

You can test the vigor of true open-pollinated seeds by planting them in large groups (1,000-2,500) in a sunny spot with good drainage and room for spreading out. In about 5 to 7 days, you should be able to tell if the seeds are viable.

3. Germination tests

If you have saved a selected, genetically modified, or hybrid seed that has not been tested for germination, you can determine if it is still viable by conducting a germination test. The test is simple and easy to do; once you have grown your plant from the seeds, you will know how many of them germinated and became viable plants.

This can help determine whether your seed is still good or if it should be discarded for the next growing season. It also helps you understand how to properly store the seeds if you want to keep them for another year.

The following information provides guidelines for germination tests so that you can decide which seeds are viable:

a. Protect your seed from contamination by other plants or insects, and rodents in your garden.

b. Conduct germination tests immediately after harvesting the seeds or ordering new seeds, as there is a time limit on the length of time for which mature seed can be stored and how long it will remain viable for.

c. For each seed packet, grow only one type of seed at a time in separate flats or pots. If you have several different types of seeds in one flat, you won't be able to identify which seeds are viable if they all germinate.

d. Do not discard the soil from the flats where your seeds have germinated. The soil and roots will help maintain the viability of the remaining viable seeds.

e. Spread your remaining viable seeds out on a folded sheet of paper, like a newspaper page or an old catalog, and store them in a dry area such as a closet or basement until germination season for your plant comes around again next year.

f. You can test the viability of seeds in your garden to check for germination faster and more effectively than by waiting to see if they grow. To do this, duplicate spread rows of seed at a spacing of 1' (30 cm). The goal is to provide even sunlight and water to all seeds in each row.

If you want to keep several seeds for planting next year, you will need different test rows for each type to have four rows or groups for each plant.

g. During the growing season, check for germination every few days and remove any unviable seedlings or planted seeds.

h. You can also use a germination test to determine if a particular type of seed is viable for planting at different times of the year. For example, you might want to know if true open-pollinated tomatoes can germinate before or after the spring frost date in your area. To do this, plant two types in separate rows at staggered intervals throughout the growing season. You will need two different kinds of tomato seeds in each row: a true open-pollinated type and a hybrid type.

It can take several growing seasons for both seeds to germinate. By the end of the season, you will be able to determine which seed won't germinate until sometime in spring, usually before the first frost date.

4. Soil tests

Another way of testing a seed is by soaking it in water for about 8 hours and then checking for germination in about 3 days (remember to keep the soil around your seeds separate from other plants or insects so that any unwanted spores that might spread from your plant doesn't contaminate your seed)

5. Paper towel test

Sometimes you may want to save seeds that don't have a clear coating. In this case, you can use a paper towel test to test for germination. Line a flat with paper towels and moisten them with a spray bottle. After several days, check for seeds that have sprouted through the paper to see if they are viable.

6. Soaking in water overnight before planting

Another simple way of checking seed viability is by placing the seed in water overnight. Seeds that remain dry at the top and do not absorb moisture will not germinate during the growing season; therefore, you can discard those seeds without wasting money on plants that won't survive past their first season of growth.

Soaking in water will not kill the seeds, but it will typically make them more receptive to germination.

7. Inoculation of seed with bacteria and fungi to kill dormancy

If you wish to save seeds from a fruit that has not germinated, spread the seed thinly on moist paper towels or cotton cloth. Cover the seeds with a thick and nutritious soil mixtures, such as garden compost or worm castings. Leave the seed(s) for one week, remove it from the mixture and place it in a glass jar with air holes on its lid. Allow the seed to sit for a few days, then put the jar in a warm place at a temperature of about 80 degrees F. After several weeks, the seed should begin to sprout.

There are several different ways of checking viability; each is suited to a certain type of seed. Knowing how and when to check viability will help you get a better harvest or ensure that your seed will not waste.

If your seeds do not germinate, they are dead, and you should properly dispose of them by placing them in a location where they will not be eaten by wild animals (such as a compost pile) or on mulch near compost piles.

Activating seeds

Activating seeds is a form of germination technique that has been used in horticulture since at least the 1930s. The activation process increases the viability of the seed by removing the storage protein and its associated water-soluble compounds through evaporation, thereby reducing their viscosity and increasing their rate of germination. It is an inexpensive way to improve the viability of your seeds.

There are different techniques when it comes to activating seeds. Some techniques can be applied to all kinds of seeds, and others are suited to specific seeds.

Few things you need to remember when activating your seeds

1. Make sure your seeds haven't been treated with chemicals or waxes that could inhibit germination.
2. Activating does not remove hard seed coats; it affects the embryo inside the seed, so you may still need to soak or scarify the seed coat before planting if it is very tough.
3. If you use a microwave to activate your seeds, make sure that none of them have been damaged by heat or have wet spots that could lead to combustion while they are being activated.
4. Be aware that the best results come from activating seeds in small groups, so you can properly monitor them.

Ways of activating seeds

1. Drying

Activate seeds with a drying technique known as stratification or dehydration, which involves placing seeds in either moist or dry environments for some time to allow them to:

- Adapt to their new environment.
- Lose moisture from their seed coat.
- React chemically with enzymes that will eliminate internal inhibitors to germination.

The word stratifies from the Greek word στρατιώτης (stratiotes), meaning "soldier," and refers to the fact that seeds were first observed to germinate in layers of moist soil.

The technique of drying seeds has been used since the 1700s by gardeners who wanted to make sure their seeds would germinate when they needed them to.

There are lots of different ways that you can use a drying technique, but most of them are based on one of these three techniques:

1. Warm Drying (cold stratification)

Warm drying is a moist-cold temperature fluctuation. It's considered the best method for activating most seeds, and you can use it for almost all kinds of seeds. Warm drying starts with soaking your seeds in water, then putting them in a warm dark place (70–75 °F) for a week or two. After that, store them in the refrigerator or another cool, dry location until they're ready to plant.

2. Cold Drying (warm stratification)

Cold drying is moist-warm temperature fluctuation. This method is used for soils that generally have a warm and cold period. You must put the seeds in a place where the temperature stays between 42 and 50 °F for 2–4 months, then return them to cold (33–40 °F) for 2–4 months before planting.

3. Warm Drying/Cold Drying (simulated winter conditions)

This method imitates natural winter conditions by putting seeds directly into cold temperatures without any previous soaking in water. It is sometimes used with species native to areas with long, cold winters, such as "Iris" or "Primula" species.

Seeds you can use drying techniques on:

- Poppy Seeds

- Sesame Seeds
- Caraway Seeds
- Sunflower Seeds (But only if the seeds have not been treated with fungicides)
- Pumpkin Seeds
- Parsley and Celery seeds (You don't need to activate these two types of seeds because they are in a dormant state, which is natural for their species.)
- Aromatic herbs such as basil, tarragon, and dill.

Some seeds have an impermeable seed coat, which protects the embryo. The seed coat's job is to preserve the embryo's life inside until the right conditions are met for its germination when it breaks through its shell.

If a seed has an impermeable seed coat, you must remove it before planting or using any activation techniques.

2. Soaking

While some seeds can be activated by drying techniques, others need to be soaked first before you can use them. Soaking seed is a process where the seed is placed in water and then left for some time, usually in which the seed will sink to the bottom due to its weight.

Soaking seeds usually has two purposes:

1. To change the soil temperature to a level where the seed can germinate.
2. To help soften the inside of the seed and remove any inhibitors to germination that exist inside the embryo.

These two factors are why soaking your seeds could be beneficial when using a certain drying technique with certain types of seeds and is sometimes necessary if you want to use a particular drying technique with other kinds of seeds.

There are three main ways to use a soaking technique:

1. Warm Soaking (cold stratification)

Warm soaking is used for species that adapt better when placed in a warm environment without the cold germination inhibitors. Warm soaking is the most common type of seed activation and has proven to be the most effective method for eliminating internal inhibitors to germination.

2. Cold Soaking (warm stratification)

Cold soaking is used for species that thrive in cold temperatures. These seeds require an incubation period where their germination is stimulated by a warm period followed by a cold one. Cold soaking requires 2–4 months in cold temperatures, and the seeds should be soaked before going into the cold period.

3. Warm/Cold Soaking (simulated winter conditions)

This technique imitates natural winter conditions by putting seeds directly into cold temperatures without any previous watering in water. It is often used with species that are native to areas with long, cold winters.

Soaking seeds take a lot of time, so you will have fewer germinated seeds than if you used a different drying technique. However, the technique of soaking seeds is much easier to control and gives you more germinated seeds at the end.

Seeds you can use soaking techniques for are:

- Tomatoes

- Beans
- Cucumbers
- Parsley and Celery seeds (This is a bit of an exception because although these seeds are in a dormant state for most of their life cycle, they are in a non-dormant state when planted outside.
- Peas
- Carrots
- Beets
- Corn
- Beetroot
- Onions
- Strawberries
- Garlic and other Allium family members (There are two types of garlic, hardneck and softneck. Softnecks can be planted outside, but hardnecks must be kept in a greenhouse.)
- Green Chiles and bell peppers (These two types of chiles can only be grown in greenhouses or a protected area outdoors.)
- Radish seeds
- Basil, tarragon, and dill seeds
- Fennel seed
- Lettuce seed
- Chives (Chives are also an exception. Although they are in the same family as onions, they aren't in a dormant state when planted outside because they still require cold temperatures to thrive.)
- Allium seeds (There are three types of alliums: leeks, chives, and garlic. They can be grown outside but must be kept indoors for the first 30–40 days after planting.)

How to use the soaking technique

Step 1: Choose the right seeds.

Determine the species and variety of seeds you'll be activating, as well as whether the seed coat needs to be removed.

Step 2: Prepare your growing area.

Make sure that your soil has the right temperature before you begin soaking. The temperature must be between 40–45 °F (4–7 °C). Use a thermometer to check the soil's temperature at least ten days before planting seeds.

Step 3: Do some research.

When researching how to activate your seeds, try to find information on specifically activating your seed species since they may differ from other seeds in their family.

Step 4: Soak your seeds.

This will be done in a moist environment as with the other drying techniques. Normally, you would put your seeds into an empty jar and cover it with a damp cloth or paper towel. Ensure that the seeds don't dry out because they will not germinate if they are dry. Also, keep the jars in the dark place where they can receive high levels of heat and moisture.

Step 5: Plant them outside... (or into a greenhouse).

After soaking, plant your activated seeds in the soil outside or in a greenhouse.

If your seeds have an impermeable seed coat, you must first remove it before planting or using activation techniques. Here are some tricks used to get seed coats off.

1. They can be soaked for longer periods.
2. They can go through a dehydration wash process instead of performing underwater conditions (like in step 4.)
3. You can put them into hot and cold air conditioning systems for larger periods (20–40 days.)
4. You can also put them in a chemical preservative (like Bordeaux mixture.)
5. You can even use a microwave oven to get the seed coats off if they are stuck on there.
6. You can remove the cotyledons from your seeds and change the periods of soaking and heating.
7. If all else fails, plant them in a more controlled environment, such as a greenhouse or a plastic bag, for one to three months before transplanting them outside.

To grow plants, you need a medium that supports photosynthesis and keeps the roots of your plants alive.

These same soaking techniques can be used if you want to use a different drying technique with a certain species of seeds that need their internal inhibitors removed to germinate.

3. Peeling

Peeling is used to removing the seed coat as well as any inhibitory substances found within the seed. Peeling is not a drying technique but a non-drying technique. Peeling works by disrupting the cell wall of a seed, which allows access to its interior and breaks down any inhibitors (such as the coating) contained inside it.

The best way to peel seeds is to either use a tool or do it manually. The idea is to use light pressure, your fingers, or a piece of gauze for the seed coat to separate from the embryo.

Ways you can peel your seeds

1. Manually (Finger peeling)

You can use your fingers to hold the two sides of the seed and apply pressure until the seed coat separates from the embryo. This technique is best used for thin-skinned seeds, such as lettuce and poppy seeds.

2. Using a tool such as a spoon

You can use a spoon to hold the seed in place and use the other hand to peel it. This is an effective way to peel thick-skinned seeds, such as beans and squash.

3. Using an apparatus (Peeling machine)

The best way to do it with thick-skinned seeds is to use a peeling machine. Technically, this is where you should start if you want to increase your germination capacity without damaging your germinated seeds. There are several peeling machine models, but they all work the same: they grind the seeds against a metal surface while shaking them.

The average time to peel thick-skinned seeds is 10–15 minutes. Using a manual technique may take you a couple of hours if you're using a manual technique.

Before the seed coats dry, one of the easiest ways to remove them is to do so before they dry. The best way to dry them before peeling is by air drying techniques such as airing out or using a fan, reducing the drying time from two weeks to a few days.

Seeds you can use peeling techniques for are:

- Pumpkin
- Squash
- Tomato
- Columbine
- Cardinal flower
- Pepper - seeds or peppers themselves can be used
- Quinoa
- Bighead bluestem
- Sesame
- Millet
- Radish - seeds or seeds can be used
- Chia
- Oats - seeds or oats themselves can be used
- Soybean

To activate your seeds with the peeling technique, you must follow the activation process:

Step 1: Make sure your seeds are dry.

This is important since it will take you a lot of time and effort to peel them if they are not dried beforehand. Use air-drying techniques like airing out or using a fan to shorten the drying time from two weeks to a few days.

Step 2: Soak your seeds.

This will be done in a moist environment as with the other drying techniques. Normally, you would put your activated seeds into an empty jar and cover it with a damp cloth or paper towel. Ensure that they don't dry out and don't get too wet either because they will not germinate if they are too wet. Also, keep the jars in the dark place where they can receive high levels of heat and moisture.

Step 3: Plant them outside... (or into a greenhouse).

After soaking, plant your activated seeds in the soil outside or in a greenhouse.

To grow plants, you need a medium that supports photosynthesis and keeps the roots of your plants alive. These same drying techniques can be used if you want to use a different peeling technique with seeds that need their internal inhibitors removed to germinate.

One important thing about peeling is that it will always work better with thin-skinned seeds than with thick-skinned ones. There are several physical properties of plant cells and some chemical properties related to the seed coat to understand why this is.

To achieve maximum germination rates and high survival rates, you need to have the right environment. The key is to keep your seedlings in a warm, moist environment where they will not dry out.

There are some tricks you should know about:

1. You must avoid direct sunlight during this time. This will dry out your seedlings, which will make them lose their roots and die.

2. Avoid cold drafts or drafts of warm air that can move around outside; the seeds will dry out too much.
3. Avoid placing the seedlings near a heat source such as light bulbs or heating vents.
4. If you have several germinated seeds, they should stay in an environment that doesn't expose them to extreme temperatures or erratic weather patterns (such as storms or high winds)

Peeling is a great way of breaking down the seed coat, removing any inhibitors, and creating the perfect conditions for germination. In addition, peeling your seeds will increase their survival rates by increasing their resistance to unknown elements in the soil and their survival probability.

While peeling methods are not very efficient at removing all inhibitors and enhancing the germination capacity of your seeds, they are the most effective method out there, and you should use them when you need to. On top of that, it's easy to follow, so if you want to get your seeds started as fast as possible, then this is the way to go.

4. Husking

Husking is the process of breaking an ear or husk free from seed and making it ready to be planted. It is one of the oldest ways to harvest seeds and can be used with many seeds. The husking process is widely used in Sub-Saharan Africa, where some populations were removed from agriculture and only kept very small herds of animals.

This technique works well with many other crops, including grass, fruits, root crops, and legumes.

Few important factors that should govern your husking process:

1. Drying

Seeds should never be soaked for more than 24 hours before husking them. If some are soaked for more than 24 hours, they will either rot or be in a watery state that makes it hard to husk them.

2. Storage

When storing your seeds, you should never put them in plastic bags or seal them. Before storing the seeds, make sure they are completely dry; this will allow them to last up to two years without losing their germination ability.

3. Warmth

Remember that you must always keep the seeds warm, so place your seedbed on top of a radiator or use a heat source of some kind during the night and day (if you live in cold places) to keep them warm.

4. Moisture

Never place your seedbed in an area with a lot of moisture. It would help if you controlled the humidity adequately. Otherwise, your seeds will rot. A good way to control the humidity is by placing a couple of layers of plastic bags on top of each other to prevent any moisture from escaping through the gaps.

5. Inhibitors

Grain husks and seed coats are the main germination inhibitors in many seeds, especially in cultivated crops like cereals and legumes. Therefore, you should remove them before planting so that you don't inhibit their germination capacity when they sprout.

Steps you should take to remove inhibitors before planting your seeds:

1. Crush them to remove the husk.
2. Soak them for around half an hour so that they absorb water and expand and open their cells, making it easier for you to remove the inhibitors.
3. When soaking, do not filter out the water through a sieve or anything like that because there are still some inhibitors in the water; instead, use your hands to press down on top of the seeds so that all their components are mixed in a mushy lump, where it is easier for you to get rid of any inhibitor by rubbing into it with your fingers until they are gone.

When husking your seeds, make sure not to break the seed into smaller pieces. This could damage them, so you will want to use a husking tool specifically designed for this task. This tool should be made from wood or plastic (not metal) and have a curved blade that is thin enough so that it doesn't damage the seed.

In addition, some tools can handle multiple types of seeds at once by having one hand holding down or squeezing on top of the seeds and the other hand swinging up and down while releasing the pressure and contacting the seeds.

Some also have a hole in the middle to pour water into it when you are husking your seeds; this way, you can dunk them into and out of the water while keeping them separate from one another, which will help to rehydrate them more effectively.

6. Flotation

Flotation is a method of getting rid of many impeding structures in your seeds. It makes it easier for germination to occur by letting just the right amount of water and oxygen get through their tough outer coating. It is especially useful for small seeds such as cress and lettuce seeds, but it can also be used to help larger seeds (like beans) if you aim to get rid of their seed coats.

Select a big container for you to submerge your seeds in and small enough so that the fluid does not overflow. Once you have selected a container, pour water into it, and move it around until the water level rises above the seeds so that they are fully covered. Once this is done, plant your seeds into the soil mixture and leave them for about one week in a warm place before retrieving them and planting them again. It would help if you always kept them underwater until you are ready to put them in soil; otherwise, they will dry out and become harder to germinate.

When picking seeds from your flotation water, it is important to be careful not to pick any seed that looks like it has a tiny piece of something sticking out of its shell (a foreign object). This could be an impeding structure.

Seeds you can use the husking technique for:

- Lettuce seeds
- Garden cress seeds
- Bean sprouts (if you want to remove the seed coats)
  - Coconut seeds
  - Chickpea seeds
  - Sesame seeds

- o Nigerian yam seeds (you can also husk and sieve them from stem parts).
- Other examples of plants that are commonly husked:
  - o Grains (wheat, maize, rice, millets)
  - o Legumes (beans, soybeans, peas)
  - o Cereals (wheat and maize)
  - o Nuts (cashew nuts, groundnuts)

Step by step process for husking technique

Step 1: Choose the correct plant seed

You should check for seeds that are mature and ready to be harvested. This can be done by either counting the number of days from when the seed was planted or checking if the fruit has matured.

Step 2: Prepare the seeds.

Prepare the seeds by removing any leaves from them. This is so that they can grow properly in their new environment. Soak the seeds in water for a short time before husking so that their cells are expanded to make the task of husking the seed easier. This increases their ability to absorb water, making it easier for you to remove their inhibitors. The length of time you soak them depends on their size; larger ones need less time while smaller ones will need longer soaking periods. Every day, change the water until it is clear; this will help to remove any inhibitors of germination inhibitors, allowing your seeds to grow more easily.

Step 3: Put the seeds in a bucket

Use a big enough bucket to submerge your seeds and small enough so that the fluid does not overflow. Once you have selected a container, pour water into it, and move it around until the water level rises above the seeds so that they are fully covered.

You can leave them under there for up to a week before retrieving them again. Keep them submerged until you are ready to plant them in soil; otherwise, they will dry out and become more difficult to germinate.

Step 4: Prepare the soil.

Moisture and organic matter should be abundant in the soil. You can use one part sand, one part vermiculite, and one part peat moss to make it. Also, add about 10% of compost and other ingredients such as fertilizer (greenhouse grade) to help with nutrients. Mix all these ingredients until they are evenly distributed throughout the soil so that your seeds can grow effectively.

Step 5: Plant your seeds

Make sure to plant the seeds at a depth of twice their size. You should also leave about 2 inches between rows for walking on and bending; this will give them room to grow.

After planting, water them and keep them near a light source. Following the light in an east-west direction is best since it will not direct your seeds towards the sun, which will help to protect them from dehydration.

Step 6: Keep watering and checking for impeding structures

Water your plants at least twice daily for approximately three minutes each time, using a watering can with approximately 5 gallons. You should also check on any inhibitors that may be located on your seeds; if you notice any foreign objects, you should remove them immediately. You should also check for germination inhibitors with a magnifying glass; you can use this to identify where both seeds have the same morphology (shape of their seed coat).

Husking is a technique used to remove impeding structures from plant seeds. It is effective because it allows the water and oxygen needed for germination to pass through the seed coat. This will also help to remove any germination inhibitors that may be present on the seeds. This is especially useful for small seeds such as cress and lettuce seeds, but it can also be used to help larger seeds (like beans) if you aim to get rid of their seed coats.

CHAPTER 7.1: GROWING SEEDLINGS

Growing your seedlings is a simple way to get started with sustainable gardening, and it doesn't require a lot of time or space. Getting them started is easy, and before you know it, you'll have lots of beautiful plants in the ground and ready to harvest.

If you're ready to get started with sustainable gardening for your home but aren't sure where to begin, there are a few things you can do to get started right away.

How to grow seedlings

Getting your seeds to sprout is not that difficult at all, even if you're starting in gardening. And when you have a nice little crop of seedlings growing, it can be the perfect time to start some compost.

What medium to use?

There are a lot of mediums that you can use for growing your seedlings, from dirt to gravel and other things. But as a beginner, you should keep in mind that what you use affects how well your seedlings grow and for how long they will last.

Here are some examples of medium you can use:
1. Dirt

If you're starting, dirt is one of the easiest mediums. It's probably not the best way to go in the long run, but it is cheap and easy to get started with.

2. Sand

Another medium you can use is sand, but you must remember that it's not 100 percent sterile. So, make sure you sterilize your medium by boiling it or filling it with clean water, free of any chemicals or residues. If you're planning on growing fruit trees or other plants that need a lot of water and want to ensure enough drainage, sand may be the medium you will want to use.

3. Coconut fiber

Coconut fiber is a good choice as you can use it as compost for your seedlings, and then come harvest time, you can use it for your garden. The same kind of coconut fiber product used for potting soils can also be used in topsoil mixes.

4. Perlite

Another one of the best mediums you can use is perlite. When using perlite, make sure to mix it with a lighter medium so that your soil does not get too light and airy. It's also important to remember that when you're using perlite, you will have to water the plants more often, and the seeds must be planted deeper than with other mediums.

5. Rock wool

Rock wool is a good medium to use for your seedlings. You can buy it quite cheaply and in bulk from gardening stores and the like, but if you want to get the real deal that has fertilizer, trace elements, and micronutrients, you will have to check out garden centers. The best way to use rock wool is to put it in a trash bin to place weights on top of it. Water does not flow under the rock wool as easily.

6. Paper cups

One of the cheapest mediums you can use is paper cups. You can buy them in bulk, and they are a pretty good option to use. The only problem with paper cups is that the surface area is small, so you will have to transplant them soon enough. If you don't, your seedlings will start growing sideways, and you might end up with long cucumbers.

7. Commercial seed starting mix

Another medium that people use for seedlings is commercial mixes and soil conditioners. These mixes cost more than dirt, but they almost always contain organic amendments like worm castings, compost, peat moss, perlite, or vermiculite (or both).

8. Gro-blocks

Gro-blocks are another option for using as a seedling mix. These are blocks that contain a starter mix, which is made from peat moss and perlite. The advantage of using gro-blocks is that you do not have to add anything else to your mix since it has everything your plants need from the beginning.

Using a medium will depend on the plants you will be growing, how many seeds you want to grow at once, and how much time you can afford to spend caring for them.

Conditions to encourage seedlings to grow

The conditions you need to have in place when you're growing your seedling will depend on the kind of seeds. Some seedlings require a cold period, others require a hot period, and still, others will be fine if they are exposed to warm temperatures and light.

Things to consider encouraging seedlings to grow

1. Temperature

Like with lighting conditions, seedlings need different temperatures to grow. Many seedlings will grow best in a hot temperature with just a little chill in the air, while others need some cold from time to time to get them growing and thriving. You will have to observe your plants and make sure that you care for their needs.

Some seeds need cold temperatures to start germinating, while others will not germinate if exposed to cold. The right temperature for a seedling to encourage growth is within 50 degrees Fahrenheit.

Some seeds will not germinate while they are wet or exposed to light. The right temperature for a seedling will depend on the seed. For example, some seeds need to be exposed to light to germinate, and others need a dark period when it's just dark outside.

Seeds should start growing at about 95 degrees Fahrenheit (35 Celsius) and continue to grow until the temperature reaches 50 degrees Fahrenheit (10 Celsius).

Some seeds will not develop properly if exposed to light for too long such as corn and lettuce, which need about 12-hour in total darkness every night.

When planting seeds, it is important to have a good mix of warm, moist conditions and colder temperatures to give the seedlings the best start possible.

2. Lighting

Lighting is important for seedlings as it helps them get their energy from the sun. Make sure that you give your seedlings just enough light to get their daily photosynthesis from the sun. As the seedlings grow, they could also die if they are not exposed enough to light.

How much or how less sunlight is needed?

The amount of light that a seedling need will depend on its stage in growth. Larger seeds and those that have just been planted will need lighter than those already germinated and growing.

The amount of light that the seedling needs will become clear once the first leaves appear. Light conditions will become even more important once the plants get their first set of true leaves.

Here are some numbers to consider:

1. Very young seedlings, including those that have just sprouted – 6-8 hours of light a day
2. Seedlings in the first 2 leaves – 8-10 hours of light a day
3. Plants that have 2 to 4 true leaves – 10-12 hours of light a day
4. Plants that have 4 to 6 true leaves – 12+ hours of light a day
5. Plants with 5 or more true leaves – 16+ hours of light a day

Some seeds need a golden period before germinating, so these will also depend on that.

You can use an app, and place sensors on your seedlings to learn more about the light conditions and how much irrigation your plants require. You can then monitor their needs in digital form and in real-time.

3. Watering

Seedlings need water to grow properly. When you start growing your seedlings, it's important to know how to give them the right amount of water, or else they might die from dehydration or algae overgrowth caused by excess watering.

Watering your seedlings will depend on the kind of seeds you're using, how many of them you have, and what medium they are growing in. Some will only need to be rinsed with water, while others need deep watering.

Consider this when watering

1. You should be watering your seedlings once a day, but make sure the water is not flooding the containers; to avoid damaging the plant's roots. The right amount of water will depend on the size of your container, compared to the size of your seedling.

2. If you're using a plastic bag to grow your seeds and transplants, then it's important not to flood them when watering because that can cause fungal diseases and diseases that are spread by the fungus "bloom" that the plant can get.

3. Using peat and perlite-based medium, you should use enough water to distribute it evenly throughout the container without leaving any dry spots. This is important because the peat and perlite will stay dry at the bottom. This problem can be solved with some moistening solution.

4. When using soil-based mediums, it's important not to overwater your seedlings, especially at an early stage of development, since they can die from waterlogging.

5. When they're first planted, seedlings need between 1/3 to 1/2 of the soil they are planted in. As they become older and bigger, they will need less water, and you can consider watering them just once a week.

6. Plants grown in a hydroponic system must have nutrient-rich water with the right pH levels that are made up of both oxygen and hydrogen.

Watering your plants should be done in a way that will let the medium drain out properly. This is because if the water stays too long on top of the medium, it will stop draining, and algae will pile up at the bottom, getting into your seedlings.

4. Natural supplements to aid growth

Seedlings need some extra nutrients to develop properly and to have a good start. You can do different things to give them extra strength, all of which work for different kinds of seeds.

Several suggestions to get you started:

1. Molasses

Molasses will give your seedlings the carbon dioxide they need and some carbohydrates that will help them develop. Molasses is a good source of phosphorus and potassium and helps to get rid of excess nitrates in the soil.

2. Seawater

Seawater works as a natural fertilizer and will improve the soil where your seedlings are growing. It's also a good potassium, chloride, calcium, and magnesium source. Seawater can also help control excessive nitrates in the soil. You should be careful not to use too much salt since it can be toxic for your seedlings.

3. Coffee Grounds

Coffee grounds have a lot of nitrogen and phosphorus, which is great for plants that are sensitive to temperature changes, such as tomatoes, peppers, and strawberries.

4 Stone Dust

Stone dust is a good source of calcium and magnesium and will help improve the medium where your seedlings are growing. It's also a good way to increase water drainage in the containers where you're growing them, making it easier for them to get enough water.

5. Green Tea or Black Tea

These teas can help develop seedlings, especially during an early growth stage. They will provide extra nitrogen, which is essential at this stage, and some vitamins that are essential for plant growth. Green tea can also be used as an organic weed killer and protect plants against pests such as aphids and caterpillars.

The brew from the tea contains abscisic acid, a natural chemical that can prevent a plant from growing too fast. Since seedlings tend to grow quickly when you're starting with your seedlings, the tea can help slow them down by giving them just enough nutrients, so the plant has time to develop properly.

6. Blood and Bone Meal

These two fertilizers are great for organic gardeners since they add phosphorous and nitrogen to the soil where your seedlings are growing. They will also release nutrients slowly over an extended period, so they won't disturb the normal growth cycle by giving too many nutrients at once.

7. Chemical Fertilizers

Although this is not something you should use to give your seedlings extra nutrients, you can use chemical fertilizers for other reasons. For example, you can spray some on the seedlings to make them grow in an emergency, but don't overdo it. Too much chemical fertilizer will kill the plants or poison the roots. It would help, if you use these once a month If used more often it will then affect your normal fertilizer cycle and cause unnecessary plant damage.

8. Plant and animal fertilizers

Animal fertilizers like rabbit manure, guano, and worm castings can also be used. They contain many nutrients that your seedlings need to develop properly but remember to be respectful of the environment and use them in moderation, to avoid contaminating the soil or water by using too much.

Seedlings are important in growing a sustainable garden, but getting the desired results, requires patience and utmost care. Growing seedlings can be hard work, but it's worth the effort your plants will be healthy.

If you have tried growing seedlings and had problems with them, it might be a good idea to start again with some more resilient seeds that are easier to take care of.

It can be difficult to learn how to grow seedlings because it is a skill that is contingent on numerous factors beyond your control, but with patience and dedication, you will get the hang of it.

CHAPTER 7.2: TRANSPLANTING

Mastering the art of transplanting is one of the most important stages of gardening. Transplanting is moving a seedling into a bigger container than the container in which it was planted. This is done when the root system of certain vegetables can't get enough nutrients from the soil.

This process is also called "hardening off" and helps plants get used to strong winds and different climates, which is especially important if you plan on planting them outdoors. If you want to grow your vegetables, it's important to learn how to transplant them in a way that will make them strong enough to fight pests and bad weather.

When to transplant

Some plants are ready to be transplanted almost immediately after germinating, while others will need some time to grow. Some seeds can be transplanted after being planted, and others can only be transplanted in the spring or fall.

Different plants should be treated differently according to their chosen type of transplant. To give you an idea, here are some examples:

1. Annuals

Annuals are one-year plants that should be planted as soon as possible in the summer. These plants must be placed in a container or row where they will get enough sunlight and ventilation. Another option is to build a greenhouse for them to grow in since they can make their heat using the energy from the sun.

Examples of annuals include:

- Radish
- Tomato
- Peppers
- Eggplant
- Broccoli
- Spinach
- Lettuce
- Cauliflower
- Chard
- Lettuce Mix
- Cucumber

Annuals should be transplanted before the temperatures get too cold to help keep them growing. Do not transplant if the plants have already been hit by frost. It will stunt their growth and prevent them from producing flowers and pods.

2. Perennials

Perennials are plants that live for several seasons and should be transplanted in fall or winter. The idea is to move them into a larger container when their roots start to grow. They will need more nutrients to avoid losing energy, and their leaves will need all the energy they can get during this process, so it is important to provide them with everything they need. The biennial category has plants that can germinate outdoors but need some time to develop roots and survive cold winter temperatures before being planted indoors or outdoors again. The second phase of these plants needs to be started indoors in late spring or early summer when they're at their optimal temperature so you can get the best results from them.

Examples of perennials include:

- Beans
- Rhubarb
- Asparagus
- Lettuce, spinach, and other leafy vegetables.
- Pole Beans
- Apricots
- Peaches and Pears
- Squash, pumpkins, and gourds
- Watermelon and Melon

Perennials should be transplanted in fall or winter and placed in larger containers with better drainage. Perennials will need more nutrients than annuals since they will be growing for several years.

3. Biennials

Biennials are plants that germinate in the summer and live their first year outdoors but must then be brought inside to survive the winter temperatures. Their second year is spent outdoors, so they need to be moved into a bigger container before winter sets in to avoid root damage due to excessively cold temperatures outside.

Examples of biennials include:

- Peas
- Tomatoes, peppers, and eggplants
- Radishes and beets
- Lettuce, spinach, and other leafy vegetables.
- Carrots, Broccoli, and other brassicas
- Potatoes, Jerusalem artichokes, and Beets
- Zucchini, Squash, and Pumpkins.

- Watermelon.

Biennials are most likely to take root in a larger container with good drainage since they will need to be watered frequently in the summer. They should be transplanted late enough in the season so that roots have started to develop before the summer heat arrives in late summer & fall.

Care for a newly transplanted seedling

A newly transplanted seedling needs special care to adjust to the change in temperature and keep growing normally.

1. Water your plant regularly but don't overdo it.

You don't need to give your plant enough water to drown it – just enough to keep the soil moist. If you use drip irrigation, you might want to water every two or three days since this system distributes water over a longer period than watering a plant manually.

You should gradually increase the amount of water your plant needs to grow and expand, and you should do so by testing the soil before letting the plant soak it up. Keep in mind that excessive water will end up causing damage to the roots, just like over fertilizing will damage your flower garden. Watering a seedling too much can also cause mold to grow and get on the soil, which is undesirable since it can affect the quality and taste of your vegetables.

They must be kept in a humid environment when growing plants, from seedlings to plants. Seedlings need this environment because it helps with cell growth, allowing them to establish their soil roots and expand their leaves. Just make sure that your seeds don't take up too much water; otherwise, they can drown and die before they even have a chance to start growing.

Transplants and seedlings can sometimes be over-watered or under-watered. This could cause the plants to die, so you must keep an eye on the plant's growth and adjust if necessary.

Transplanted seedlings should be monitored closely, even if you think the soil is the perfect moisture level for them. These plants will need to adjust to their new watering schedule and system, which might mean your plant isn't getting enough water but doesn't look like it yet.

2. Give your plant a full spectrum of nutrients.

Regardless of the type of transplant you're doing, you should give your new plants all the nutrition they need to grow and survive. Plants will not produce as much and taste better, if not properly nourished.

Your newly transplanted seedling will be stressed, so it might stop growing or spread out its leaves to fix itself – this is called "going into shock." Take special care to give your plant the nutrients it needs.

Nutrition needed for a newly transplanted seedling includes:

1. Calcium – This is needed to help the roots' natural expansion.
2. Iron – This is often the main nutrient for "seasoning" vegetables.
3. Potassium is needed to ensure healthy cell growth and development.
4. Phosphorous – Similar to calcium, phosphorus works with potassium in helping cellular structure and functioning.
5. Sulfur – This is essential in promoting cell growth.

6. Water nutrients – Nutrients like chlorine, zinc, manganese, and more are needed to ensure proper hydration by the plant and its roots.

A well-balanced soil mix is needed before transplanting seeds or seedlings. This will include all the nutrients above and nitrogen, boron, and magnesium, which can help support healthy root growth and development, respectively.

3. Make sure your newly transplanted seedling gets enough light.

Most plants will need enough light to encourage growth; however, some plants rely on a certain amount of sunlight to complete their first development phase.

Whether the plant is a seedling or a transplant, it should be positioned where it will receive the amount of light it needs. Seedlings and transplants should spend at least six hours a day outdoors, though they can go up to ten hours or more in the shade.

If your new plants are indoors, position them in a warm area with lots of light and good ventilation. Position them beside windows, near any heaters or heat sources, underneath grow lights in your house, etc.

Plants should be positioned close enough to these light sources to receive enough heat and light, but not too close to any heaters or heating sources since this can cause them to burn. They're also better off in a drier area than a humid one.

4. Take good care of your transplanted seedling roots.

These roots are its vital organs, so you must take extra care of them until the plant gets used to its new schedule and environment.

Your newly transplanted seedling roots will most likely experience damage from the transplant process even if you have done everything correctly – wait for them to grow out. Plant roots are sensitive, so they'll have to adjust to their new environment.

If you notice your seedling's root system is damaged or showing signs of rot, you should use a fungicide or an anti-rot solution (such as copper sulphate) to help the root system recover. Alternatively, you can cut off some roots with a knife; if the remaining roots are still alive and healthy, they'll grow back after two weeks.

5. Watch for signs of transplant shock.

This happens when a plant is moved from one place to another and experiences environmental shock. Transplant shock can last from two days to several months, depending on the size of the transplant and for how long it was growing at its previous location.

Other factors that go into the duration of your plant's departure from healthier conditions include:

1. The size of your transplants - small plants will take less time to adjust compared to larger plants which require more time. Ambiguous sizes like medium or small plants can sometimes take longer, too.
2. The amount of damage to the plant during the transplanting process.
3. If your seedling or transplant roots were severely damaged, too.

You cannot do much to help your plants recover from transplant shock since they need time to adjust; however, you can fix the problem if it isn't too severe. Therefore, you'll need to take extra care of your plants (see above).

Prevent problems with your transplanted seedling by starting with healthy seeds and proper planting conditions.
This includes:

1. Choosing seeds and soil with high germination rates.
2. Ensure the seeds are planted in the right type of soil, at the right depth, and in a well-drained area.
3. Make sure your seeds and transplants are not exposed to any harmful chemicals like fertilizers, pesticides, etc.
4. Take precautions to protect your seedlings from pests like insects and birds while growing outside and exposed to predators of all kinds during their development – even after transplanting them.

Transplanting is a very delicate part of gardening. The newly transplanted seedlings are extremely sensitive and require extra care. Good germination is essential before planting; root damage could occur if the crop is planted too quickly. The plant roots need time to adjust to their new environment after transplanting. Badly damaged root systems often result in dead plants, so you must take extra care in transplanting your seedling.

How to transplant
Step 1: Prepare your soil.

Make sure that you prepare your soil to absorb water well. Root development is dependent on good soil. Otherwise, the plant will not be able to absorb nutrients. The next step is to check the PH level of your soil. The pH should preferably be around 5.5-6.5 and above, for your plant's roots to be healthy and strong enough to grow without damage.

Step 2: Prepare your plant.

After preparing your soil, the next step is to prepare your plant. Start by removing dried leaves and other green parts on the stem as they will block plants' roots from absorbing water and nutrients. The next thing to do is check if any insects or other bugs in the area can affect your plants. Additionally, you should check for pests beneath your plants or in nearby areas to nip the problem in the bud before it starts to grow.

Step 3: Digging holes and placing the plant

After you have prepared your plant, it is now time to dig holes in the soil where you will put your transplanted plants. Ascertain that the hole is deep enough for the transplants to absorb water easily. A good size hole or pot should be around 2~3 times bigger than the transplanted plant in its original pot. Next, put your seedlings into the hole you made and pull out the soil from behind it, so it's well anchored in place. Finally, fill up some of your soil back to stay firmly in its place, and start watering it regularly.

Step 4: Transplanting your seedlings

If you have decided to transplant your seedling, it is now time for you to do this step. Before transplanting, ensure that you are familiar with the species to determine whether the plant can handle the transplant or not. Following that, you must ensure that there is minimal damage to the plants' root systems. If there are insects or pests on your plant, they can cause damage to its roots, resulting in dead plants. Nowadays, many tools and gadgets are available in the market which help us dig small holes in our gravel without disturbing them to avoid soil entrapment and root injuries. This can also reduce the disturbance factor on the seedlings.

Step 5: After transplanting your plants

After you have finished transplanting your seedlings, make sure that you place them where they are exposed to direct sunlight but not in a place where they will be exposed to hot temperatures. These plants need to have indirect sunlight as it helps them grow and absorb nutrients efficiently. Also, make sure that you water your transplanted seedlings regularly so that they can absorb water easily from their surroundings, grow healthy, and strong.

If we take proper care of our transplants and use the right tools, we can reduce up to 98% of damage to their roots even after transplanting them.

Often, seedlings damaged by transplant shock may show browning, or wilt shortly after being transplanted. This is because the plant's roots were traumatized during transplanting and can therefore not absorb water or nutrients correctly for the plant to grow healthy and strong. If a plant shows signs of gray mold or lichen on the stem after being transplanted, it indicates a root rot problem that should be treated immediately to prevent further growth problems in your plants.

CHAPTER 8: GROW MEDIUMS AND URBAN GARDENING TECHNIQUES

There are a lot of gardening techniques that don't require manipulating the soil and instead grow plants from seeds. This chapter explains these methods and how you can use them to grow vegetables for your home or small farm.

Coco Coir

It is one of the most popular grow mediums, especially for outdoor growers. Coco coir has excellent water retention and air-holding characteristics, which is ideal for hydroponics.

Coco coir comes in two forms:

1. Chipped pieces of coconut husk

This form is harder to work with because you must rehydrate them before using it.

Chipped coconut coir works best with large plants like raspberries and tomatoes because they won't completely break down in the soil and clog up your drainage holes.

2. pre-hydrated bricks or "coir bricks."

Coir bricks come pre-soaked in a large block and are ready to use straight out of the box. It's easier to work with than chipped coconut coir because it's already soaked; you need to crumble it up and add it to your growing medium.

Advantages of Using Coco Coir

1. Good water retention qualities

It doesn't hold water as well as peat moss, but it holds a lot more than commercial potting soil. It can lose water over time depending on the size of your container, but you can add water to keep it in good condition.

2. Protection by coco coir

Because coco coir is made of fiber and not clay, it doesn't absorb all the harmful chemicals in your soil and environment. This means the plants will be more likely to grow healthy and produce better, thus, it is ideal for growing seedlings or young plants.

3. Good aeration

Coco coir allows for good airflow in your pots or grow beds, which is good for plants that require more air or those prone to diseases.

4. Restorative and slow release of nutrients

Coco coir is made from coconut husk, a renewable resource easy to process and treat. Most nutrients will be released slowly into your potting mix and bloodstream, meaning you don't need to fertilize every week. If you're growing outdoors, it will take longer to attract pests and diseases because the coco coir isn't giving off a lot of nitrates, unlike peat moss, which contains a lot of organic matter.

5. Easy to maintain

You can add more coco coir when you start to run out, but it's not necessary. Unlike topsoil and compost, you don't have to add too much because it will puff up in the pot or grow bed if you over-fill it. If you want more insulation, use more coco coir instead of planting in plastic pots or layered gardening with many pots and many soil layers. It will also retain less moisture when compared to other types of growing mediums because it doesn't hold water unlike peat moss or potting soil.

6. Renews and restores soil

After your harvest, use the coco coir to renew your soil. Add it to the compost pile or mix it with your garden soil. It will reabsorb water and nitrogen, thereby improving the overall health of your garden bed.

Disadvantages of Using Coco Coir

1. Vastly different moisture requirements

Coco coir is not like potting soil or topsoil in that it does not have to be watered constantly throughout the growing season. However, once you plant your seedlings, you will need to water them regularly as they lose water through their roots and over time. The first week has the lowest water requirements, while the third week has the highest. You must also avoid overwatering since it can cause root rot and damage your plants.

2. Fragile plant roots

The biggest disadvantage of using coco coir is the huge amount of coir you will need to grow your vegetables. It is not recommended that you grow in small spaces because coco coir only works with large plants like tomatoes and raspberries; smaller root vegetables can't handle being grown in coco coir without dying sooner or later.

3. Nutrient depletion

Unlike growing your plants in soil or compost, coco coir does not release nutrients into the soil for your plants to use. You still must add a lot of fertilizer for the plant made solely from coconut husk to grow well and produce plenty of fruits and vegetables. You'll still need to add fertilizer periodically, so you'll need to spend more time searching for a composting service or doing your own composting.

4. Larger growing container

For the same reason as #3, you must use a larger growing container when growing plants in coco coir. Because it's not made from soil or compost, building your container will require more work because you won't be able to use the same methods with soil and compost.

5. Difficult to handle

Coco coir is not like other materials you can use in your gardening. It is made from the fiber of coconut husk and will break easily if you try to squeeze it or pick it up with a pair of gardening shears because you must moisten it before adding it to your growing medium. If you're not careful, the coco coir will crumble and completely disintegrate into tiny particles, which means that there will be no coco coir left for next time. This is a big problem because once this happens, you will have to re-mulch your soil manually day after day until the next harvest cycle begins.

6. Not ideal for root vegetables

There are no disadvantages of growing root vegetables in coco coir, but it's not recommended. Root vegetables are best grown in soil or compost because they need more nutrients and water than the average vegetable plant. There are many disadvantages of using coco coir for root vegetable plants. It holds too much water and makes the roots rot faster, leading to dead root vegetables that taste bad or give you food poisoning.

Coco coir is not as simple as other growing mediums because you must know what you're doing before starting, or your plant could die. While using coco coir can be risky, it is a good option for experienced gardeners who like growing fruit and vegetable gardens on a large scale. Many people use coco coir because it's environmentally friendly, so consider trying out coco coir in your garden this year if you want to avoid using peat moss.

Nutrition needed during seedling if coco coir is used

Growing seedlings using coco coir means that you need to take extra care in all your growing needs since growing seedlings under coco coir mean that you don't have to worry about when to water. Using coco coir means starting your seeds a little further in advance, which means your seedlings can reach their roots whenever they are ready.

Different nutrition that is needed when using coco coir during seedling is as follows:

1. Phosphorus

Phosphorus is a very important part of the nutrition of your seedlings when using coco coir. This is because the coco coir doesn't have a lot of phosphorus, so your plants need the extra phosphorus to grow strong and healthy. Your seedlings will need between 150–and 200 mg/L of phosphorus to grow properly. A good source of phosphorus is DAP, which you can find at any nursery or online gardening sites.

2. Potassium

Potassium is another important part of your seedling's nutrition because it is a big part of new growth, especially when using coco coir. You need 270–300 mg/L of potassium for your seedlings to grow properly and make strong roots and stems. A good source of potassium is banana fertilizer or other organic options like comfrey tea or bat guano. They will provide a good source of potassium for your plants and help make up for not having enough of the nutrient in coco coir.

3. Nitrogen

There are very few amounts of nitrogen in coconut husk, so you need to add some more nitrogen into your coco coir planters. The amount of nitrogen you need is 100–120 mg/L, which can be found in a good organic fertilizer, like fish emulsion or seaweed extract. Other sources of nitrogen include leaf mold, compost tea, and compost.

4. Calcium

Your seedlings need calcium, but it's not as high a priority as the other nutrients. Including about 40–60 mg/L of calcium is enough for your seedlings to grow properly. Calcium comes in several forms, including gypsum and lime, found at your local nursery. A good organic source of calcium would be ground eggshells or limestone meal, which are good sources of calcium to ensure your seedlings have plenty of calcium.

5. Magnesium

Magnesium is not needed as much as other nutrients, but it is still important for your seedlings to grow properly. For seedlings using coco coir, it's best to add about 10–20 mg/L of magnesium into the medium to help them grow strong roots. Good sources of magnesium include Epsom salts, dolomite lime, and manures rich in sulfur.

These nutrients are essential for seedlings and will help them to grow properly. For a seedling using coco coir, it would be best to add these nutrients before you start planting the seeds through the whole process to be fully prepared for their journey. Taking time in preparation before planting the seedlings helps ensure that they have all the nutrients necessary to grow strong roots and healthy stems.

Nutrition needed during transplanting if coco coir is used

Coco coir is very different than other growing media because it can't be transplanted between setups. There are no organic options for doing this, so you will have to use synthetic forms of the nutrients to help your seedlings grow faster.

There are several ways that you can use synthetic nutrients in coco coir planters, and they are as follows:

1. Fertilizer tea

Fertilizer tea is very important for seedlings and other plants in your garden because it helps your plants grow stronger and faster. Using fertilizer tea helps to boost the number of nutrients needed by the plant, as well as to give it more nutrition to be able to grow even more. It's also a good feeder for younger plants to get what they need and continue being healthy.

2. Compost tea

Fertilizer tea and compost tea are very similar in what they provide to the plant. They both help ensure the plant is getting all of the nutrients it needs, but compost tea also helps boost its growth and development. Compost tea is ideal for transplanting into coco coir planters because it acts as a supplement, providing nutrients to your plants during the planting and growing process. Compost tea will help your seedlings grow faster by providing them with even more nutrition, which they need for their journey as a plant.

3. Micronutrients

Micronutrients are nutrients that are normally found in high levels in the soil, but some plants don't have enough of them to grow strong or healthy. This can be very dangerous for plant life, so crop nutrition companies make micronutrient supplements to help boost the amount needed by the seedlings. You can use these supplements during transplanting if you use coco coir as a medium — completely organic.

4. Slow-release fertilizers

Slow-release fertilizers are usually tiny chunks of fertilizer or another nutrient that can last several weeks or months and are slowly released into the plant. They are very useful in coco coir because they help give the seedlings what they need depending on how long they have been in the medium. These little chunks are slowly released into the coco coir planters, keeping your seedlings strong, in preparation for its journey as a healthy plant.

5. Solid fertilizers

Solid fertilizers are another useful form of nutrients, but they can only be used in solid containers. Because you can't start adding these nutrients to your coco coir planters until the seedlings have been transplanted, it would be helpful if you are cautious while using them. It's best to store these solid fertilizers in a separate container with no other nutrients or mediums until you are completely done planting your seedlings. You will then add the fertilizer to your planters once they are finished and ready for fertilizing, which can be a helpful guide for how long it's been since you transplanted.

Comfrey tea is another great way to give your plants what they need before transplanting into coco coir planters.

Growing Your Sustainable Garden Using Coco Coir

Coco Coir is a great medium to use for starting a sustainable garden. It's a renewable resource, so it's not hard to find, and you don't have to worry about anything you are using for your plants. You can use fertilizer tea or compost tea to give your seedlings what they need for a healthy journey as plant life. Using coco coir to grow your plants will help them have a healthy life and make gardening more environmentally friendly.

While coco coir planters aren't typically recommended for beginners, it's best to have some prior experience with other plants and mediums before attempting to use them.

They are just like any other medium with multiple purposes and uses. They can be used for many different plants, like flowers, vegetables, and even herbs. It can also be used for indoor gardening. It is a great way to grow fresh food year-round without worrying about the weather. Using coco coir planters is also a good idea if you have animals like chickens or reptiles. It helps keep your plants and garden safe from animal damage or even contamination.

Coco coir planters are usually used to grow vegetables and herbs indoors because they are important parts of a healthy diet and living healthy. They can also be used for growing flowers, but it is not ideal for flowers to grow in them.

Materials:

- Coco coir
- 3/4" hardware cloth
- Plastic lid or organic potting mix
- Hose or watering bag
- Watering can or sprayer (to water your plants)
- Twine, string, or line (for hanging plants)

How to Make Your Coco Coir Planters

Step 1: You need to find enough coco coir to make at least four planters with a few inches around the edges and a couple of inches in the middle. It would help if you had enough coco coir for each planter to be about an inch thick on both sides of where you cut it.

Step 2: Cut your coco coir into blocks of about two inches long by one-inch wide. You could measure them with a ruler, but you can just cut them by hand. If you are not sure how to make a straight line, you can use two lines to mark your block so that it is perfectly even.

Step 3: Lay your hardware cloth on the table and let it lie flat so that it is straight and flat, at least as much as the height of the block of coco coir. It doesn't matter if it's even or not, if it is close to being even horizontally.

Step 4: Place your coco coir block on top of the hardware cloth to guide your placement. Cut the hardware cloth to be about an inch longer than the coco coir block, and then cut small slits in the edges to help place it on the coco coir block.

Step 5: Stack all of your planters together and place them in a container. The container should have enough room for you to fit all of them close together, but it should not be too large because they will expand when you water them. You can place a plastic lid over half of the planters to cover them up while they are growing.

Step 6: Add water to your planters once a week until the coco coir is completely saturated. Let it sit for 15 minutes and then drain out most of the excess water, leaving only a little moisture in the planter. If you notice that they are getting too wet, you can add more coco coir to your planters.

Step 7: You can start planting seeds, cuttings, or bulbs into your coco coir after watering them for at least seven days. Place the seeds in the center of a block and cover them with a thin layer of coco coir.

Step 8: If you don't have any growing medium, you can put your seedlings directly into your coco coir planters. This isn't recommended if you are using coco coir for the first time because it will be harder for your plants to grow in the coco coir before they get used to it.

Growing Your Plants in a Coco Coir Planter

Have patience when you are growing things in your coco coir planter because it may take longer than you expect. It is always a good idea to pay attention to your plants and ensure they get what they need without being overfed.

Step 1: Plant your seedlings in the center of the planters.

The seeds can be on the bottom of grow containers, but it's best to place them in the middle.

Step 2: Keep an eye on your plants as they grow.

Once they have sprouted, they should remain close enough to their roots to receive moisture and nutrients from them as needed. It would be beneficial to water them every day or every other day, depending on how quickly or slowly your plants grow in your coco coir planter.

Step 3: Add some organic potting mix

After the coco coir has been growing for a week or two, add some organic potting mix over the top of your plants. This will help keep the coco coir from drying out as it grows.

Step 4: Put a soil block.

When your plants are about two inches tall, you can put a soil block between the soil and the coco coir. It's best not to fill them with soil because it'll be difficult to get them out when watering the planter.

Step 5: Water your planter frequently.

Check your coco coir planter every day or every other day for a few weeks to make sure you're watering it when it's needed. If you can't do this, the plants may not be getting enough water and may die from rotting.

Step 6: Cut your plants' roots back to only about three inches long (if they are longer, they could damage their roots).

Step 7: When you notice that your plants are too tall for your planter, you can transplant them into a larger container.

You don't have to move them immediately if you want to keep growing them in the same container. They can be planted up to around twelve inches apart in bigger pots than their original coco coir planters.

If you are transplanting your seedlings, put a large block of coco coir under the bed of soil to give them enough space to grow. When your plants have sprouted and grown a little more, you can move them as usual.

Coco coir planters are an ideal way to grow vegetables indoors, and they make a great gift for anyone considering eating healthy foods.

The coco coir used to make the planters is an inexpensive material that is easy to find even in small quantities, so it won't cost you very much if you have several planters growing at once.

CHAPTER 8.1. HYDROPONICS

Hydroponic gardening is a technique for growing plants without the use of soil. It's a year-round method for growing a variety of edible plants indoors, regardless of what Mother Nature has in store for you outside your door. A hydroponic system doesn't take up much space (unless you want it to), it can be used almost anywhere, and plants grow faster than they would in the ground. It's easy to see why hydroponic gardening is quickly becoming a popular way to grow plants in various settings, including kitchen counters and university dining halls.

The Greek word "hydro" means "water," and "ponos" means "work." The water does the work in hydroponic gardening—in this case, delivering nutrients to the plant roots.

Advantages of Hydroponics

1. Can Be Placed Anywhere

Hydroponics is appealing because it is simple to set up and can be used almost anywhere. It requires little space, making it ideal for small yards and limited growing space.

2. More Control Over Growing Environment

Another major advantage is controlling all aspects of your plant's environment and adjusting these as needed. This means you can control temperature and lighting, and grow plants at any time of the year or through any season. You can also control humidity and water, which gives you a lot more booming control over the life cycle of your plants.

3. Maximizes Growth

Because you can adjust the soil, air, and water, your plants can grow to their maximum potential. This means you can grow a lot more food in a container than using traditional gardening techniques.

4. Small Space Garden

Hydroponics are the ideal solution for you, if you live in an apartment or condo that lacks a garden space. You can use small containers that are easy to maintain and place them anywhere there is sunlight. A small container garden like this requires very little work to maintain; however, the rewards are plentiful — often including fresh vegetables and herbs that you can cook with and enjoy.

5. Grow a Variety of Plants

Additionally, you are not required to grow only one type of plant at a time. You can mix and match plants in the same container. They will all thrive together—even vegetables that require different types of growing environments (like tomatoes and lettuce) can be grown with no problem. This means you can customize your plants as you like while saving space, time, and money on supplies.

6. Good for Beginning Gardeners

The ease with which hydroponics can be learned is one of its most appealing features. It's possible to find affordable equipment online and in gardening supply stores. You can also find plenty of books and tutorials on the subject, so you don't need to be an expert gardener to start using a hydroponic system to grow plants.

Disadvantages of Hydroponics

1. Expensive

You might find it difficult to get started using a hydroponic system on a tight budget if you're starting. It is possible to spend a significant amount of money on plant growth equipment and supplies. If you choose to do so, make prudent investment choices — remember, the investment will pay off in the long run.

2. Limited Growing Space

Because you don't need much space for a hydroponic garden, it can be difficult to grow enough plants at once to feed an entire family all year round. It requires more room for an extensive system; however, a small container garden will provide you with plenty of fresh vegetables and herbs for use at home. This makes it a good choice if you don't have the space to maintain a traditional garden.

3. Maintenance Required

A hydroponic system is more work than some other gardening methods because you need to add nutrients and check the pH levels regularly to ensure your plants are getting what they need. This means you can spend hours every week working in your garden, which might not be suitable for everyone—but it's worth it when you sit down to enjoy homemade produce with your family in the winter months.

4. Other Plants Only

Some hydroponic systems are designed only to grow certain types of plants. It's possible to find one that will accommodate many plants, but it's not as easy as traditional gardening. This means that you can better control the environment and protect your plants from common plant diseases.

5. Not for Everyone

A lot of people don't like hydroponics because they don't want to spend a lot of time in their garden. It takes a lot more work than just putting some soil and fertilizer in a container and waiting for the seeds to grow.

While hydroponics has been used in greenhouses for decades to grow fruits and vegetables, it can also be used for indoor gardening.

Starting Your Own Hydroponic Garden

Step 1: Find a Location

Find the spot where your hydroponic garden will be located. This may be a countertop in your kitchen, a balcony, or an indoor garden in your home. Make sure it receives an adequate amount of natural light. A south-facing window is ideal, but any window will do. You can also place a hydroponic garden in your yard, provided that the plants you want to grow will be able to thrive there.

Step 2: Choose Your Plants

Choose the type of plant you want to grow in your hydroponic garden. This may be a vegetable, herb, flower, or small tree.

To name some of the common plants to choose for hydroponics for the sustainable garden:

- **Vegetables**: Lettuce, tomatoes, cucumbers, peppers, herbs (basil and cilantro in particular), greens

- **Herbs:** Mints, oregano, parsley, cilantro

- **Flowers:** Zinnias and marigolds are especially easy to grow

- **Small trees:** Dwarf citrus trees like kumquats may need special attention, but they can be very rewarding.

Step 3: Decide on Your Hydroponic System

Hydroponic systems come in a variety of configurations:

Nutrient Film Technique (NFT)

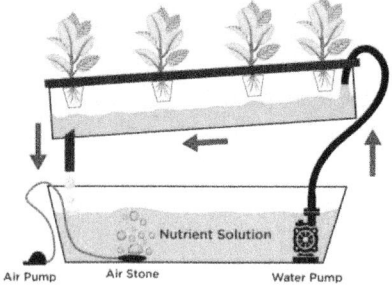

The nutrient solution is pumped into channels that can hold a variety of plants in NFT hydroponic systems. The nutrient solution flows through the channel, over the plant's dangling roots, and back into the hydroponic reservoir because the channels are slightly sloped. Grow medium is rarely used in NFT hydroponic systems, and the plant is usually secured with foam net pot inserts.

NFT hydroponic systems are best for plants with a small root system, such as leafy greens, due to the size of the channels. Because of the size of the channels, NFT hydroponic systems are often used in commercial or industrial indoor gardens.

Deep Water Culture (DWC)

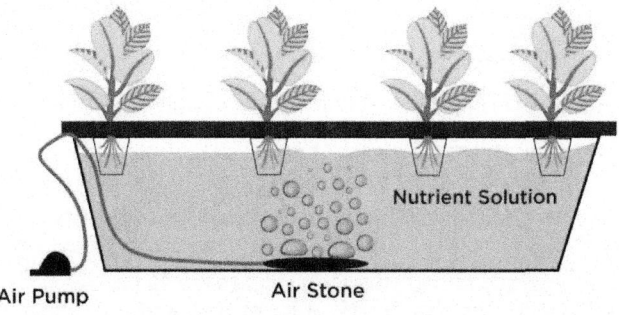

DWC is a hydroponic system that uses deep water to help plants grow. In DWC, the nutrient solution is pumped down into an area that meets the plant's roots. The nutrient solution flows in and out of this shallow water without pumps or moving parts.

Because DWC systems can be extremely expensive and are not used for very small plants, DWC is most used for large plants such as tomatoes, cucumbers, and herbs.

Ebb-and-Flow (Flood and Drain)

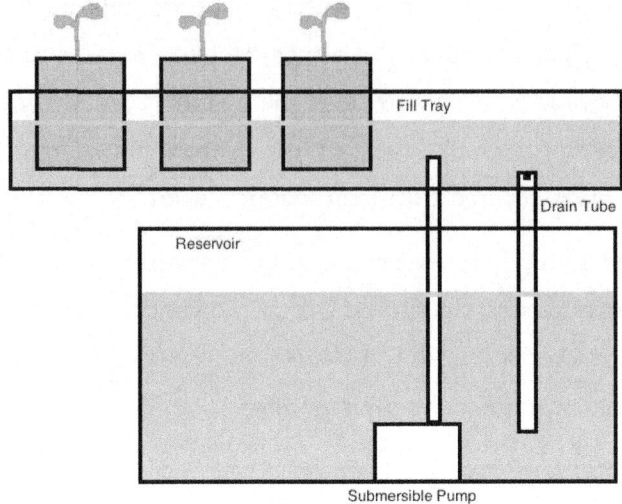

Ebb-and-flow systems are the most common hydroponic system, and they are also relatively easy to build. They are most used for small fruits and vegetables, including herbs.

In an ebb-and-flow system, the nutrient solution flows into a container that is partially submerged in water. Some nutrient solutions drain back down into a reservoir while the rest stays in the top container with the plants. This flow continues until you stop it by stopping the tubing that pumps water up into the container or by draining all the nutrients out of it. This is used for small plants or plants that don't need to be kept wet, like lettuce.

Drip System

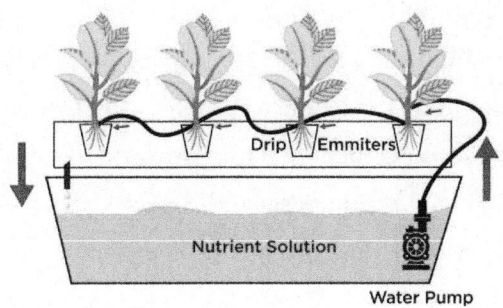

A drip system is a hydroponic system in which nutrient solution drips into the plant's container all at once. The drip system requires the least work and least technical knowledge for maintenance. It may use a reservoir filled with nutrient solution, or it may use no reservoir at all, just a small amount of water to soak the soil.

The drip system is perfect for growing plants that are easy to maintain, such as flowering plants, herbs, and high-value vegetables.

Aeroponics

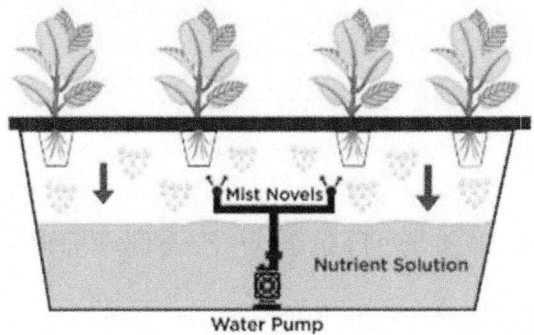

Aeroponics is a hydroponic system that allows plants to grow in an airy, soil-less environment.

As the term "aeroponics" suggests, this method uses a pump to spray nutrient solution onto the plant's roots and into its container. Aeroponic systems are extremely complex, and they may be too difficult for beginning gardeners to use. However, aeroponic systems tend to offer the most benefits for growers: aeroponically grown plants are free of soil borne pests and diseases and can be harvested quickly after growing to maturity. This is usually used on plants like lettuce and tomatoes.

Wick Hydroponics

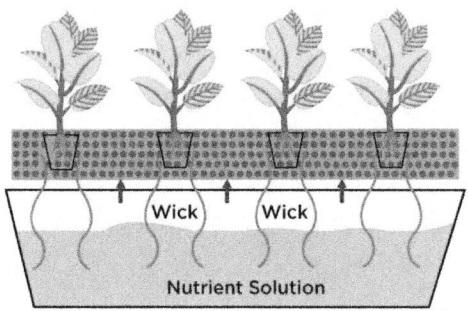

Wick hydroponics is a method of growing plants without soil.

In wick hydroponics, the plants' roots are held in the air, or a net of trays filled with wet sphagnum mosses. The idea is that the roots stay moist and healthy by absorbing moisture from the mosses. This is usually used on plants like herbs and small tree seedlings.

Step 4: Choose A Light Source

The optimal light source for your hydroponic garden is determined by the type of plants you intend to grow.

- For flowering plants, like zinnias and marigolds, use grow lights to make sure that they flower as quickly as possible.

- For leafy greens and herbs, use fluorescent lights to promote healthy growth and prevent leaf deterioration. Hydroponic gardens need an artificial light source since they do not produce nutrition. This can be a simple incandescent bulb or a more complex fluorescent tube with adjustable intensity. Fluorescent lights are often used for specific light colors because of their low energy consumption and high lumens per watt ratio.

Step 5: Choose a Hydroponic Grow Medium

Before starting your hydroponic garden, you'll need to decide what type of growing medium you want and what will work best with your system. The type of growing medium you should use is determined by the plants you'll be growing as well as the hydroponic system you'll be using.

There are numerous growing mediums available, each with its own unique set of advantages:

Rockwool

Mineral wool made from molten rock and slag is called Rockwool. It absorbs water easily and holds it for a long time, allowing plants to use the water slowly as it is needed. Rockwool will not break down over time like peat moss. Rockwool has long been a popular hydroponic grow medium, especially for starting plants or clones. Before using, it must be pH balanced.

This is accomplished by soaking the cubes in a pH-balanced solution. Because Rockwool is designed to allow optimal airflow for plant roots, it's critical not to squeeze the cubes. Rockwool is a porous medium made mostly of rock that has been heated, melted, spun into strands, and then shaped into cubes, blocks, or slabs. Rock wool can be found online or at a local hydroponics store.

Oasis Cubes

Oasis Cubes are another popular hydroponic grow medium. They are made from continuous looped fiber, can absorb water and hold it for long periods.

Oasis Cubes offer a combination of the best of both worlds—the ideal water-holding capacity of rock wool, and the faster nutrient uptake of porous media. Oasis Cubes are made from a special paper pulp type that forms a dense, closed-cell structure that does not absorb water. The cubes also provide direct access to air and nutrients for roots, via air pockets.

Hydroton

Hydroton is a very fine aggregate of volcanic rock. It reduces the plant's root zone and can hold up to four times as much water as other rock types.

Hydroton is also very difficult to clean and has a bad odor that can permeate the whole room. This makes it suitable only for small-volume hobbies or educational activities.

Hydroton's most practical use is in growing small plants like herbs and vegetables in weakly-acidic soil—the general idea here is to keep the pH of the root zone at 6.8 or below.

Hydroton can be purchased at hydroponic stores and online.

Additives are often added to hydroton to speed up the rooting process, produce better root growth, and protect young plants from disease. Additives include ammonium sulfate, nitrate mineral salts, and trace elements like iron, manganese, and boron. There are also increasingly popular additives that feed plants with specific nutrients like N-P-K (nitrogen, phosphorus, potassium), amino acids (for example, acetyl-lysine), and vitamins A&D (for example, thiamine).

Coco Coir

It is one of the most popular grow mediums, especially outdoor growers. Coco coir has excellent water retention and air-holding characteristics, ideal for hydroponics.

Coco coir is a dense material that works well in hydroponic applications. It holds water very well, which means that plants irrigated with coco coir don't need as much water to grow as those irrigated with other types of growing media. However, you can successfully use coco coir along with a drip system if you are diligent about watering once a week.

Coco coir holds a lot of water, which means that it may have a drainage problem under the hydroponic garden. As a result, plants irrigated with coco coir need to be watered frequently. Moreover, coco coir is not easy to clean; you must use strong chemicals or dish soap so as not to clog your plant's nutrient system.

Coco coir comes in two forms: heavy and light. The light form of coco coir is denser and will drain faster than the heavier form.

Rock Phosphate

Rock phosphate is also a great alternative to Rockwool. Rock phosphate comes from fossilized animal and plant life and has a high concentration of phosphorus and potassium.

Rock phosphate holds onto water well, but not as much as clay pellets. The perfect amount of drainage with Rockwool is critical for hydroponic systems that use the ebb-and-flow, flood-and-drain, or deep-water culture systems. However, rock phosphate does not hold water unlike clay pellets, so it may better suit drip irrigation systems.

Rhizotonic Soil Nutrients

Rhizotonic nutrients are a great alternative to chemical additives for coco coir, Rockwool, and another soil-less media. They provide the perfect balance of macros and micros while keeping fish and crustacean parts out of the equation. This is critical because these materials can lead to root rot in hydroponic systems or contaminat runoff water if grown in soil systems. This is especially important for organic hydroponic gardeners! Growers should also be aware that there are regulations on the transportation of organic matter through multiple states, so it's not recommended to use them if you plan on shipping your harvest across a state border.

A hydroponic growing medium can be made of a variety of materials. Anything that a plant can grow in, including air, is considered a medium (Aeroponics). While securing the plant into your hydroponic system, hydroponic grow mediums must allow both oxygen and water to reach the roots. Unfortunately, there is no definitive answer to which hydroponic grow medium is the most effective. It takes a lot of trial and error to figure out what works best for you.

Step 6: Buy Nutrients & Supplements for Hydroponic Plants

Hydroponic nutrient supplements are used to provide what a plant needs to flourish. There are three categories of nutrients: Nitrogen,

Phosphorus, and Potassium. These nutrients are added to the water in the hydroponic system.

Nutrients for Organic Hydroponics: Flourish N-P-K

Flourish N-P-K is a perfect organic growth supplement for the soil-fewer growing mediums listed here. Flourish's balanced formula has all the nutritional needs that a plant needs to thrive and grow. This is a complete hydroponic fertilizer with all essential elements required for plant growth, including N-P-K (nitrogen, phosphorus, and potassium). It also contains calcium, magnesium, sulfur, and iron.

Flourish makes an excellent growing medium for any kind of plant. It's a highly concentrated food for plants mixed with water and oxygen to create a nutrient solution. Flourish has been formulated specifically to meet the nutritional needs of plants grown in soilless media like rock wool or coco coir. Using "thoroughly mixed" fertilizer solutions is important when working with soilless mediums. Solutions become increasingly concentrated as they travel further away from the solution reservoir.

Nutrients for Hydroponic Plants: Flora N-P-K

Flora is another great organic growth supplement for hydroponics. Like its competitor Flourish, Flora has a balanced formula with all essential nutrients required for plant growth, including N-P-K (nitrogen, phosphorus, and potassium). It also contains calcium, magnesium, sulfur, and iron.

Flora's formula has been specifically designed for hydroponic growing because it is one of the few organic nutrients that can supply a strong N-P-K nutrient solution. It is great to use if you are looking to grow plants quickly or have questions about the health of your plants.

Flora contains fish and kelp as its dietary supplements. Fish and kelp contain omega fatty acids, which are a great source of natural nutrition for plants. Plants need these omega fatty acids just like we need vitamins in our diets.

Nutrients for Water Pumps: Metro-Mix

Metro-Mix is a perfect nutrient for hydroponic systems. It can be used to start seeds, as Sprout Recipe, or as a fertilizer. This product is "Metro-Mix" because it provides all the elements required by plants such as macro and micronutrients such as N, P, and K, along with trace elements such as Zinc (Zn), Iron (Fe), Manganese (Mn), Copper (Cu), Acid Phosphate (AP) and Potassium (K).

For hydroponics, Metro-Mix is especially useful because it helps prevent the browning of roots from using too much potassium nitrate or too high a pH level. It can also help prevent calcium and magnesium deficiencies in hydroponic systems.

Step 7: Purchase A pH Meter & pH Up/Down

Using a pH meter is the only way to read your plants' specific pH levels. Hydroponic gardeners use pH meters to maintain balance in their nutrient solution. This prevents many problems in hydroponic systems, including algae growth and root rot diseases.

Purchasing a pH meter is an important step for any hydroponic gardener. You'll be able to monitor and correct your system's pH levels before they become an issue.

Step 7.1: Ways to Measuring the pH Level

When it comes to hydroponic gardening, maintaining a proper pH is one of the most important tasks. A plant can only take in minerals if the pH of the nutrient solution is within a certain range. While the ideal pH range varies depending on the plants you're growing, most plants thrive when the nutrient solution's pH is kept between 5.5 and 6.5.

It's not difficult to determine the pH of your solution.

There are three ways to determine the pH of your hydroponic nutrient solution:

1. Litmus Test Strips to Measure Hydroponic pH

One of the cheapest ways to check the PH of your hydroponic nutrient solution is to use litmus test strips. When dipped into your nutrient solution, the strips contain a pH-sensitive dye that changes color. The pH reading is then determined by comparing the strip to a color shade chart.

Because the color differences between test strips can be subtle, measuring pH with them can be difficult. It's less accurate as a measurement because it's sometimes difficult to tell what color the strip is giving. You can still get a good idea if the pH of your hydroponic nutrient solutions is in the right range.

2. Electronic Meter to Measure Hydroponic pH

Using an electronic meter is another option for measuring your solution's pH. This method works because it can measure the electrical current in the nutrient solution to determine the pH levels. You can then compare the current reading to a color chart or a table of pH levels to measure your solution's exact pH level.

191

Electronic meters are useful for checking the pH of your nutrient solution because they can provide reliable measurements of your nutrient's specific pH levels.

3. Hydroponic Bubble Test to Measure Hydroponic pH

Another way to measure hydroponic nutrient solutions is with a hydroponic bubble test. This test can tell you the actual state of your solution and how acidic or alkaline it is.

A hydroponic bubble test works like a hydroponic soil test. However, it will also tell you the exact pH level of your nutrient solution. How does this help you?

All plants commonly take up minerals if the pH levels are right to absorb them. If your nutrient solution has too high or low a pH level, then most nutrients will never get absorbed by your plant. As a result, they won't grow very well and eventually die from a lack of nutrients.

Step 8: Mix & Add Nutrients, Start your system

The final step in getting your hydroponic garden up and running is to get everything started. Fill your system with water and run it to make sure everything is working properly. This is a crucial step because you want to catch any leaks as quickly as possible. Mix your nutrients and wait 15 minutes before testing the pH to know if everything is in order. You'll need to adjust the nutrient solution's pH and make any other necessary changes. After that, add your plants to the system and set your grow light timer to the amount of light your plants require.

Step 9: Keep an Eye On Your Plants.

Now that you've done all the hard work, it's important to keep an eye on your plants. You'll want to check your hydroponic system at least once a day for the first week or so. As a result, you'll have quick access to any necessary adjustments. If you catch an issue early, then there's less of a chance that something will go wrong.

To help prevent light leaks and nutrient deficiencies, be sure to monitor your plants regularly. Each type of plant has its own special needs for water and light.

To sum it up, there are many different factors involved in growing vegetables in a hydroponic garden. However, you'll need to buy the right equipment and nutrients for your system before you can get started.

After that, you'll need to choose what type of system best suits your needs (small space or large space) and how to use the equipment you purchased. Last but not least, you'll need to learn how to select and use the right nutrients, and additives for your plants.

CHAPTER 8.2: AQUAPONICS

Aquaponics is a growing method that involves growing fish and plants in the same space. The waste from the fish is converted directly into nitrates by the bacteria in the surrounding area when using this growing method. These nitrates are used as plant food before the remaining water is returned to the fish, free of harmful contaminants. This results in a nitrogen cycle that is both effective and efficient.

Though the waste can eventually become toxic to the fish in the tank, the bacteria introduced to the water converts the waste into beneficial nitrates before any fish are harmed. While the aquaponics farming and growing method are simple, there are a variety of systems to choose from, including the Nutrient Film Technique.

Aquaponics systems can be placed inside a Hydroponic Garden or on top of one because the indoor environment does not concern water's salinity. The outdoors does not suffer from high temperatures.

The Differences Between Aquaponics vs. Hydroponics

Even though hydroponics and aquaponics are highly effective plant-growing methods, there are some key differences to consider before deciding which is the best option. Because both methods can grow plants without soil, they can be useful to you if you want to avoid using soil. However, you will need to devote time to learning about the method you select, so understanding the differences between the two options is critical.

The following are the primary differences between aquaponics and hydroponics:

1. Cost of chemical nutrient

As discussed in chapter 8.1, chemical nutrients are required in hydroponic systems, which can be very expensive. These nutrients have also become scarce in recent years, driving up prices even further. The fish feed used in an aquaponic system, on the other hand, is much less expensive.

2. Limited control of plants

Because of the high concentration of chemical nutrients in a hydroponic system, you have little or no control over how quickly the plants absorb them. This can be a problem because it can cause the development of various medical conditions and diseases. On the other hand, aquaponic systems use a natural method of cultivation, which gives you full control over plant growth.

3. Cleanliness and efficiency

Aquaponics systems are much more efficient than hydroponic ones, especially since both soil-free growing methods use only about 10% of the water that traditional agriculture needs to produce the same results. The fish waste in the latter method is often disposed of in a nearby sewage system, but this can be a huge problem for the surrounding water supply because it can often lead to algal blooms. On the other hand, aquaponic systems use the nitrogen-rich waste from the fishes and convert this into beneficial nitrates used as food for the plants. While this fertilizer may seem tiring to use at first, it is only used every three to four weeks and produces a steady amount of food for your plants.

4. Soil-free growing methods

Aquaponics systems only require a small amount of grow medium to do their job. All that is required is a small amount of fish waste and water fertilizer, both inexpensive and readily available.

5. Bacteria used with either method

One key aspect of aquaponics is the bacteria needed to convert fish waste into nitrogen-rich food for plant growth. Beneficial microbes are typically cultured in laboratories from commercial varieties. They are available for free or very low cost to most farmers with a suitable soil base for their crop.

6. Time commitment required

The learning curve involved with aquaponics is lower since it only involves learning how to obtain the right amount of fish feed and maintain the right nitrogen and oxygen levels in the water. On the other hand, hydroponic systems are more complicated since they require a lot of time and effort to regularly monitor soil pH levels and pesticide use. This extra work can often prove too difficult for many people.

7. Environmental sustainability

Nutrient-rich fish waste from aquaponic systems is used as fertilizer by its surrounding plants instead of being poured into a nearby drain with many hydroponic systems.

8. Natural method of growing plants

The soil used in aquaponics systems is made of fish waste and water that has filled the crevices left over from the fishes' hideouts, which allows the soil to circle the roots of the plants without needing to be compacted. On the other hand, hydroponic gardening relies on peat moss and vermiculite, which must be regularly monitored and managed to prevent any nutrient deficiencies. Another advantage of aquaponics is that it uses fish waste as a natural source for fertilizer, making these systems more environmentally friendly than some hydroponic methods that use chemical fertilizers.

9. Additional uses of aquaponics

Aquaponics systems can also produce useful products, including tilapia fish, prawns, and vegetables. To grow these plants, all required is a small amount of space and time. On the other hand, you are limited with what hydroponic systems can grow since they require different soil.

Starting Your Sustainable Garden Using Aquaponics

Once you have decided that aquaponic gardening is the best method for you, it's time to select the necessary tools and equipment and begin setting up your system.

Drawbacks of Aquaponics

1. Cost of the Equipment

The growing beds and fish tanks used in aquaponics systems can be rather expensive, especially if working with a smaller system. It often takes years before farmers return the initial investment. While you may be able to find some cheap alternatives for these items, they may not provide adequate benefits. The plants grown with hydroponic methods are usually dramatically smaller than those in an aquaponic system since the soil and nutrients used in aquaponics methods are more concentrated.

2. Less privacy

Because of the increased amount of water used for watering, hydroponic systems are often susceptible to fungus problems and pests, which are not usually an issue with aquaponics. On the other hand, you must be aware that the fish feed can sometimes attract unwanted visitors like rats or cats, especially if you buy a large or complicated system. The water levels must also be monitored because they can rise quickly in some hydroponic systems if the pumps become clogged with debris. Since this is a problem in all growing systems, it is best to have all your equipment hooked up at one point for easy monitoring and adjustments.

3. Time needed to grow plants

Aquaponic systems require a greater amount of water to grow crops and produce food, increasing the time it takes. In extreme cases, the system needs to be fed at least once every two weeks, while in smaller systems, you may only need to feed it once a month. On the other hand, hydroponic gardening can be done without feeding your plants. Most growers usually choose this method if they want to grow vegetables and fish since they can use all the water required for fish farming and then add all their other crops using only a fraction of the water required by aquaponics.

4. Length of life for seeds

A few types of aquaponics systems may not require nutrient-rich fish waste, but hydroponic systems can still be grown using both fish and non-fish waste. This is because the exact length of time seeds needs to be in water depends entirely on the species being grown. On the other hand, most plants survive longer in the soil since it helps prevent diseases and pests from growing and harming them. The plants that grow in hydroponic systems can look similar and have the same size as when they were planted, while aquaponics systems produce smaller and weaker plants after a few weeks.

5. Hectopascals of water needed to grow plants

Aquaponic systems require a greater amount of water than some hydroponic methods because they create an environment flooded with water throughout the whole system. This produces more nutrients for the plants since they are constantly bathed in it; while those in hydroponic systems, need less amounts of these so that they can breathe freely but cannot regulate it themselves. The amount of water needed to grow crops in aquaponic systems is dependent on the size of the system and its load but will average about 200 liters for every square meter of growing area. Hydroponic gardening can be done for smaller mass production but will still require more water.

6. Necessary equipment

To cover large areas for aquaponic systems and have a deep-water system to feed veggies and fish, you will need multiple pump systems. Although this can be relatively inexpensive, it is also quite time-consuming. On the other hand, hydroponic fracking relies on very small pumps to deliver water from tanks to the plants, so this method requires minimal additional equipment. The amount of water used depends on the size of the system and your needs.

Aquaponic systems can be located indoors, outdoors, or anywhere in between. When choosing an indoor location, you will need to determine how much space your aquaponic system will need and how much sunlight it receives. It is also important to find a location that will not be affected by extreme weather conditions, such as winds and rain. If the environment becomes too cold or too hot, your plants' growth will be limited, and your system's production will suffer. Aquaponics can also be done outside in areas with high temperatures but low rainfall, like the California desert.

Aquaponics systems are not limited to just fish farming but can be used for vegetable farming instead, depending on each area of interest and set up for hydroponic gardening methods.

Types of Aquaponics

As there are many options, we'll break down the most popular types of aquaponic systems so that you will be able to make an informed choice.

Nutrient Film Technique Systems

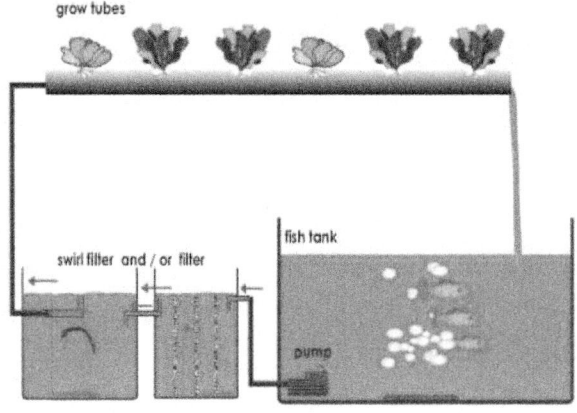

As explained in chapter 8.1, NFT systems are also known as "flavor savers" or "flood and drain" systems. They use the same water flow through the system while only continuously changing a small portion of it. The plants' roots are held in place by a water reservoir made of PVC piping that is filled with gravel or expanded clay balls to ensure proper drainage and ventilation. An inline pump circulates the water throughout the system, allowing for excellent pond water drainage and preventing the roots from becoming stagnant in a pool of water. These systems can be set up quickly and easily, require very little maintenance, and produce great yields. You should line the reservoir with at least two inches of gravel to prevent evaporation or corrosion damage to your equipment. The fishes' tank should also be completely airtight, as any leaks can allow water to evaporate due to external factors. You can grow any plant in an NFT system, like tomatoes, peppers, cucumbers, and much more, but running water is usually necessary for aquatic plants. A self-contained pond pump can provide this so that no extra work will be involved with your system. The difference between NFT systems and traditional aquaponic systems is that the plants don't need to be fed. The only thing required is water, making NFT systems a great option for organic gardeners who want to grow an entire organic food production system from scratch.

Aquaponic Drip Systems

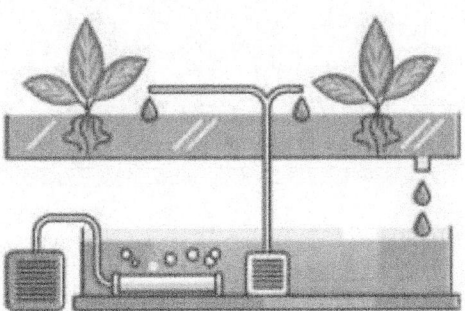

These systems are known as "tuber type" or "drip irrigation" systems. They are usually the most expensive system you can make and require much maintenance and monitoring, but they tend to produce the best

201

yields. This growing method involves a low-pressure dripper line connected to a PVC pipe with a faucet at its end. Water is then connected to the drip line by a PVC reducer, which ensures enough pressure for the water to flow through the pipe and reach all containers throughout the system. The fish tank is housed in a sealed container, but it can be easily opened and inspected to ensure that everything operates properly. The system can be constructed out of any material you want, but it is usually made from metal due to its durability. This system is suitable for growing various plants like lettuce, herbs, and vegetables and can even be used to grow fruit. The downside of this system is that it can be quite expensive, and the maintenance required for each container takes a great deal of time and effort. Any root transplanting will also have to be done manually, which may cause some problems as you don't want to damage your plants accidentally.

Deep Water Culture

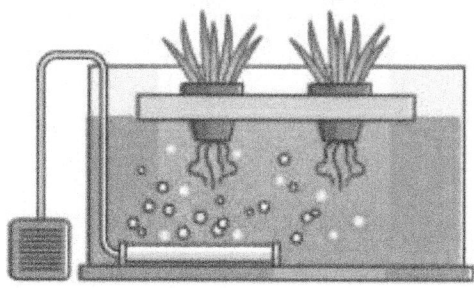

As discussed in chapter 8.1, Deep Water Culture can also be used in Aquaponic systems. These systems are made of PVC or polypropylene piping used as a raft for the plants, which are then held in place by a vertical stand and netting made from plastic. The pipes should be filled with gravel and are completely submerged in the fishes' tank, but not so much that the leaves of your plants will be inundated while they are sitting inside. This type of system doesn't require much maintenance, and it works best if you use floating plants that can withstand plenty of sunlight to supplement your system. The fish in a DWC system are fed brine shrimp to increase their protein requirements.

Recirculation Systems

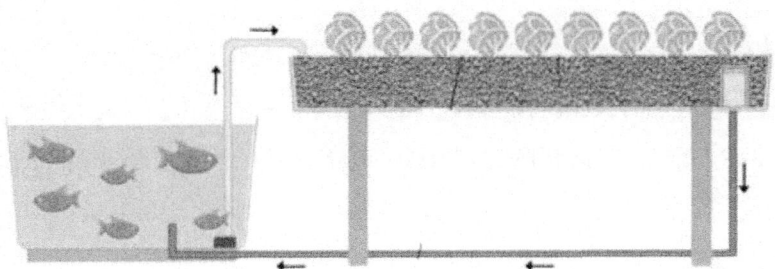

Also known as "flow-through" or "circulation" systems, this is another popular method of aquaponic gardening and is typically the most cost-effective method. These systems are built from PVC or polypropylene piping, typically with a diameter of 1-inch. The water in your fish tank is then connected to an inline pump that circulates it throughout the growing area, turning a garden bed into a mini-watering system for your plants. If you want more control over the amount of water that flows through your plants, you can also use a drip irrigation system in place of the pump. These systems tend to be less expensive than their NFT counterparts and are generally easier and quicker to build since few components are needed. All that is required is drilling holes in the PVC pipe and inserting it into the fish tank. Plants can be grown on almost any type of soil, and the water is usually changed once or twice a week in these types of systems. These systems are a great choice for small gardeners since they are easy to manage and require minimal maintenance. They can also grow various plants like basil, lettuce, cucumbers, peppers, and tomatoes.

What should be in the ecosystem to promote a flourishing ecosystem?

Some things should be in the ecosystem for the plants to flourish. A sustainable garden that uses aquaponic systems should have the following things to promote a flourishing ecosystem:

1. Fish

There needs to be the right fish in a sustainable garden. The common types of fish are goldfish, bluegill sunfish, channel catfish, koi, and perch. Goldfish are a good choice for the tank because they eat all weeds and algae. Koi can also eat these things, and they help clean the tank. Bluegills are easy to control because they eat smaller fish and insects. Channel catfish are omnivores that eat pretty much anything available to them. Perch can eat mosquito larvae if there are any in the pond as well as insects or bugs, since they all can't be controlled by chemicals (bug spray) sprayed on them.

2. Organic fertilizer

There should be organic fertilizer to promote growth and health in the plants. Fish poop is a good source because it has phosphorus, potassium, nitrogen, and trace minerals. The plants will use these nutrients to grow and make nutrients, like amino acids and proteins required by the fish to digest smaller organisms available in the water for them to eat. Other things can be used as fertilizer, including coffee grounds, horse manure, blood meal, or bone meal. However, they can introduce weeds or insect larvae into your system, so it is best not to use them unless you have an abundance of materials that need to be composted.

3. Organic mulch

There are many organic alternatives to building a healthy and thriving habitat for the fish in your aquaponics system. These are natural products and do not contain harmful chemicals: peat moss, compost, seaweed, shredded newspaper, and shredded leaves. Peat moss is a good material for mulch because it holds moisture well and provides fertilizing agents, which helps the plants grow healthier and faster. Compost or manure is another high-quality organic source that can be used as mulch because they put nutrients into the ground like nitrogen instead of taking it from the water in their system like other things might do. Decaying plants and wood chips can help populate the garden by providing nutrients for the plants, helping them grow at a faster rate.

4. Water

There must be enough clean water to maintain a flourishing ecosystem. Fish are important in maintaining a healthy ecosystem as they provide food for bigger animals that eat smaller organisms that can create algae and other unsanitary materials. Therefore, it is essential to keep your fish healthy so they will provide nutrients to the other creatures in your system. Aquaponics has access to clean fresh water from the fish tank recirculated using a pump and filter throughout the garden.

5. pH of the water

There needs to be a good pH between 5.5 and 6 for optimum plant growth if you use NFT systems like raft bed aquaponics, or about 6.5

for deep water culture, depending on the plants' needs on the pH scale. This varies from system to system but can be reached by testing your water regularly.

6. Temperature

For the plants to thrive, the water must be between 60- and 80-degrees Fahrenheit (14 and 25 degrees Celsius). To maintain their optimal temperature, the fish must remain in this range, depending on their type. Fish will not thrive in extreme heat or cold, and neither will your plants. The fish tank must have a certain amount of heat so that they do not overheat. The maximum recommended temperature is 90 degrees Fahrenheit or 40 Celsius, and the optimal temperature is 80-85 degrees Fahrenheit or 25-30 Celsius. These temperatures will help keep your fish healthy and help them flourish.

7. Equipment

There should be all the equipment necessary to maintain a flourishing ecosystem in your aquaponic systems, such as filters, pipes, oxygenators, and pumps. This is essential because, without these pieces of equipment, your fish can get sick and die along with the plants due to all the waste they produce.

8. Fish food

There must be enough and the right types of fish food for the fish to thrive in your system. The common types of food are as follows: bloodworms, mosquito larvae, grindal worms, blackworms, crickets, and brine shrimp. These types of food will give them all the nutrients they need for growth and development. There are many other food sources you can use, such as broccoli, potatoes, or algae, but these can stunt their growth or even kill them if there are too many algae.

Aquaponics can be done without fish, but it is a good idea to have them in the system so you can watch your plants and fish thrive and grow. In aquaponics, you grow both by using fish waste, organic matter, and bacteria. The bacteria alive in your system provide all the nutrients needed for your plants to grow, drink water (through their roots), and receive food through their leaves. The waste created by the fish will also be used in this process when it is either recycled through a filter or broken down into fertilizer which can then be used on other plants in the garden.

Using the aquaponic system to grow your sustainable garden will give you a lot of benefits. This is an efficient way to grow your garden without using chemical products that may be harmful or using environmentally damaging products like pesticides. Everything is natural so that the garden will be healthy, and the plants will thrive and flourish.

CHAPTER 9: SOIL

The soil in your sustainable garden is one of the most important resources you'll work with. The better your soil, the healthier your plants will be, and the more successful you'll be as a gardener. There will be no success in your ecosystem without healthy soil, let alone plants. You'll never get a substantial harvest from your garden if your soil doesn't improve.

Different kinds of soil

There are different types of soils, just as there are different plants. Each type of soil has its unique characteristics. Soil is a natural resource classified into various soil types, each with unique characteristics that provide advantages and disadvantages for growing.

Identifying the type of soil required for a project is critical to ensuring healthy plant growth.

1. Sandy soil

Sandy soil is light, warm, and dry, with a tendency toward acidity and nutrient deficiency. Sandy soils are frequently referred to as light soils due to their high sand content and low clay content (clay weighs more than sand).

These soils drain quickly and are relatively easy to work with. They warm up more quickly in the spring than clay soils but tend to dry out in the summer and suffer from nutrient deficiency caused by rain.

By increasing the soil's nutrient and water holding capacity, organic matter can help boost nutrients to plants.

This type of soil is used best for small plants that require quick drying, such as annual and perennial flowers.

2. Clay soil

Clay soil is a nutrient-rich type containing more than 40% clay particles. The main advantage of this type of soil is that it retains nutrients within its structure for long periods, which makes it an ideal soil for growing plants that need to be sustained over a long period. This type of soil also helps prevent nutrients from leaching out from the soil when watered or during heavy rainfall events. Because it compacts easily and drains slowly, it can be difficult to work with, making root penetration difficult.

Working with clay soil is difficult because it tends to stick to tools and becomes very hard when wet. Breaking up this soil to make it easier to plant or turn over can take a lot of effort. Clay soils also cool down slowly during the spring and warm up quickly during the fall, which causes them to become compacted when worked with. A good way to deal with this is by using many different organic amendments in your gardens, such as compost, manure, leaf mold, and bone meal. These will help loosen up the soil, so it's easier for plants' roots to penetrate the ground.

Typical clay soil will contain more than 40% clay particles and less than 40% silt particles. It won't be easy to dig or till, but it is rich in nutrients and can be easily amended to help loosen it up. It retains nutrients for plants for a longer period and is not subject to nutrient deficiency over the long term. This soil type is best suited for heavy root feeders such as carrots, beets, parsnips, rutabagas, and potatoes.

3. Loam soil

Loam soil has characteristics of both clay and sandy soils but is considered ideal for stable growing conditions. This soil type has enough heavy particles to retain nutrients and moisture but is porous enough to allow root absorption. Loam soils also retain heat better than clay or sandy soils, warming up in the spring quickly when they are worked with and drying out slowly in the fall when they become compressed by heavier fall rains.

These soils retain sufficient nutrients to help plants grow strong roots but are not subject to nutrient deficiency over the long term.

Loam soils are also heavy, with a 60% or more moisture content. They are often known as rich, black, or mellow loam. This type of soil has a medium amount of sand and clay suspended in it, which enhances the ability of this soil to hold moisture and nutrients for plant growth, but it is still very porous. (The water-holding capacity in this type of soil ranges from 30% to 80%). Loam soil will often have a good amount of organic matter present in it as well, which will also help improve soil structure and retention.

Many consider Loam to be the best type of soil for gardening. Loamy soil with a high proportion of organic matter content contains a wide range of plant nutrients and water, making it fertile and forgiving. Other advantages include its ability to retain warmth or coolness throughout the growing season, which makes it suitable for most plants; when plowed, loamy soils are easily turned over; they are well-draining and slow to compact and form a solid soil structure that resists erosion. Loamy soils can break down gradually over time into more fertile clay loams, which is why this is the most common type of sustainable soil.

The soil quality in an organic garden doesn't have to be too different from the quality in a non-organic garden. What we add to it and how we manage it makes the difference.

Loam soil is used best for gardening, growing vegetables, and even small trees.

4. Peat Soil

Peat soil contains a large percentage of dead plant material or peat. A sustainable garden with this type of soil will have a high level of available nutrients, but not for long because the soil will get depleted at an accelerated rate.

Peat soil does not contain much organic matter, so there is no nutrient holding capacity. These soils are very acidic and can be very rocky when wet. Depending on the peat present, peat soils break down best into either a loamy, sandy, or clay loam soil type.

Soils are often called moss/peat soils due to their high plant material (moss) content, making them dark in color.

5. Chalk Soil

Chalk soil is white and found primarily in semi-arid areas, such as the Great Plains of Canada. This type of soil is relatively alkaline and dry. The calcium carbonate (chalk) content makes it a very rocky soil that erodes easily, taking out large amounts of topsoil over time.

Most plants cannot grow well in chalk soil due to its high level of pH salt. Using this type of soil for gardening may not be an option unless you lower the pH level with organic matter and add water-holding capacities with compost/manure or organic matter amendments to help prevent erosion and nutrient loss.

Chalk soils are acid in nature and should be amended with organic matter or lime/rock dust to improve the soil structure.

The kind of soil you use to grow plants is largely determined by the plants you want to grow. Plants that require consistent water and nutrients will grow best in clay soil.

Preparing different kinds of soil for successful vegetation

You can do many different things to improve your garden's soil health. Using this method of growing plants will help you create an environment perfect for growing a wide variety of vegetables and fruits.

1. Soil aeration

Over time, adding air to your soil helps it maintain a healthy structure, which improves your plants' ability to absorb nutrients, water, and oxygen. You can add oxygen to your soil using a three-pronged pitchfork or an aerator-tine tool. You can also use a rototiller in areas that haven't been tilled recently. Tilling at least once every six months is recommended if you use mechanical tools to improve your soil health. Adding air to your soil can have a lasting effect on its quality over time—especially for crops that need good drainage and aeration like carrots, squash, and potatoes.

2. Soil testing

Before you start adding amendments to your soil, it is important to know what nutrients it needs. Knowing what your garden needs will help you make better decisions about the type of soil you should use, whether to amend it, and how much to add for the best results. Soil testing will assist you in determining the precise nutrient, pH, and moisture levels that your soil requires to grow healthy vegetables and fruits. You can also use these tests for long-term planning purposes by figuring out how often and how you need to add healthy amendments to your soil over time.

The USDA's Natural Resources Conservation Service has a free online tool that can help you figure out what is needed in your soil.

3. Mulching

Mulching helps maintain a good quality of life for microorganisms living in the top layer of your garden beds by keeping moisture in the ground, preventing weed growth, and providing a buffer from extreme temperature changes. It can also help your soil retain nutrients and keep it cool during hot periods of the year. For example, grass clippings make a good type of mulch if you have access to them.

Mulch with layers of organic material like leaves and grass clippings, which will slowly decompose over time. Use several inches or several sheets of newspaper and lots of composted yard waste as mulch. Shredded leaves are lightweight and won't compact easily, making them an excellent choice for using on top of your soil to keep it cool during the summer months when temperatures can get higher than 100 degrees Fahrenheit or above.

4. Soil amendment

Adding amendments to your soil is a good way to help it maintain its fertility over time, sustain plant growth during periods of hot weather and help prevent nutrient deficiency in plants over the long term.

There are numerous types of amendments available, including the following:

1. Compost

Compost is rich in nitrogen, potassium, and phosphates (the three main plant nutrients) and is a good source of trace minerals. It supplies your soil with many essential nutrients essential to healthy plant growth that may not originally be present in the soil. Composting your soil is critical for increasing its water and nutrient holding capacity. This will make it easier for your plants to get the nutrients they need over a long period instead of getting them all at once and then leaching out with the first heavy rain. You should add about two inches of compost onto the top of your soil to create a soil amendment to work with.

2. Manure

Manure is a good source of nitrogen and phosphates and helps balance out pH levels in your soil if they are too acidic or alkaline. It's also an excellent source of trace minerals and long-lasting organic matter. This will help provide nutrients for your plants over a long period, rather than having them leach out rapidly as they would in nutrient-poor soils. Apply approximately two inches of manure to the top layer of your soil due to its high nitrogen content, which can burn your plants if applied incorrectly or in excess.

3. Rock dust

Rock dust is a good source of calcium, iron, and other trace minerals. It helps "lock in" nutrients, making them available to plants for a long period. You can choose to use rock dust if you want to improve the nutrient-holding capacity of your soil over a longer period. Rock dust is an excellent choice when your soil has high levels of calcium or iron deposits, which need to be reduced so that your plants can take in those essential nutrients over a longer period. Rock dust comes from crushed rock and has a consistency like very fine sand. Rock dust can be added as a dry amendment to your soil at about four pounds per 100 square feet. When using rock dust, do not add it until after planting because it can affect the growth rate of your plants.

4. Leaf mold

Leaf mold is a great source of nitrogen and other small organic compounds essential to plant growth. It can be used as an amendment or replacement for fertilizer at about one pound per 100 square feet. Leaf mold is a dry, fine-textured soil amendment that contains compost and animal manure. However, it usually needs to be mixed with compost before use, so it doesn't have too much nitrogen content. This amendment is often used as an addition to keep your soil healthy between fertilizer applications.

5. Seaweed

Seaweed is rich in calcium, potassium, and trace minerals. It can be used to condition your soil for plant growth by adding about two inches of seaweed onto the top layer of your soil. This will help your soil become more nutrient-rich and improve your plants' growth rates over a long period of time. Seaweed is good for improving your soil's pH levels and adding trace minerals to the root zone.

There are a lot of different amendments that can be used to change the quality of your soil, but these are some of the most popular and easiest to use. Knowing your soil's characteristics is important to pick out an amendment that will have the desired effect.

Those who want to achieve maximum soil health, improve disease resistance, and reduce maintenance can all benefit from using this method of growing plants. This method works particularly well when you are a year-round grower or plan on having your fruits and vegetables in your backyard.

Sustainable gardening: Land care

There are also many ways to help improve soil health by simply managing your garden, including some of the following techniques.

1. Let compost and mulch break down naturally.

Allowing compost and mulch to decompose naturally is one of the most effective ways to improve soil health. This process will take much longer, but it will ensure viable nutrients for your plants and prevent them from becoming a nuisance.

2. Don't disturb the beds by tilling or turning over your soil too often.

The structure of your soil is important because it helps hold nutrients inside, so disturbing the beds by tilling and turning over the soil can damage that structure. 3 to 4 inches is a good depth for tilling your garden if you decide to till so that you don't destroy nutrients in the lower levels of the soil.

3. Don't apply fertilizer during the growing season.

Organic compounds break down over time and become dissolved in the soil. When you apply nutrients directly to your soil, it may be too late for them to be absorbed by your plants.

4. Don't add too much nitrogen to your soil.

If applied as an amendment, it has a preferable effect on plant growth. Still, over application of nitrogen can cause a severe nutrient imbalance in your garden that can hurt the visual appeal of your plants and cause problems with pest and disease management.

5. Don't overwork your soil.

Suppose you are only adding organic matter to the top few inches of your soil. In that case, you don't need to worry about expelling nutrients from your garden because this material will break down and become a part of the beneficial structure of your soil.

6. Don't add too much phosphorous to your soil.

Phosphorous is needed for plant growth and can be obtained by adding fertilizer directly to the root zone, but when it is too high, it can lead to a nutrient imbalance that can harm plant health and result in unhealthy leaves.

7. Don't add too much nitrogen if there is phosphorus in the top few inches of your soil.

If you add more of either one, you will have nutrient imbalances in your soil. Too much nitrogen may cause nutrient toxicity that can harm plants, especially if there is seasonal variation in light levels.

8. Don't aerate too often.

The particles in the top few inches of your soil are important because they help form a barrier that prevents moisture loss and reduces erosion by wind. This structure will be damaged if you aerate frequently, and nutrient losses can occur.

9. Don't let your soil become waterlogged if rainfall levels are low for extended periods.

If your soil isn't well-aerated and has a lot of moisture after rainfall, this could lead to drainage problems and flooding.

10. Don't let your plants become thirsty during extended dry periods.

If your plants are getting all their water from the soil around them, their leaves could die, and they could lose important root systems needed for healthy root growth.

Taking care of your soil is a lot of work, but you can make it last longer and help improve its overall health with some simple care and maintenance.

How can chickens, ducks, and rabbits help with soil health?

Aside from the benefits of their manure and eggs, there are a few other ways these animals can help with soil health.

1. They keep away invasive earthworms by eating them.

Gardeners have reported that poor soil has turned into excellent soil when chickens, ducks, and rabbits mow earthworms.

2. They also retain moisture and prevent it from evaporating.

Chickens will use their feathers to provide shade for their eggs, helping to retain moisture in the soil when needed. Ducks and rabbits are also known for digging holes under plants to lay their eggs, preventing moisture from evaporating from the soil.

3. Good at grooming and aerating their environment.

Chickens, ducks, and rabbits will use their beaks to chew on weeds around the garden and then grind them up to feed themselves with those weeds. This process helps to keep the soil healthy by preventing weeds from taking over.

4. Fertilizing prowess.

Ducks, chickens, and rabbits are known for eating a lot of plants, thus providing them with a lot of nutrients that they can provide to the soil. These animals also excrete a large amount of nitrogen in their manure and other nutrients useful for soil health.

5. Keeps the critters away and reduces pest problems.

Wildlife such as deer and wild rabbits that were once a problem in gardens are now thought to be kept at bay by these animals' presence in the garden. Their meat tends to be toxic to these animals, making them avoid it completely when they contact it.

6. Lost nitrogen, phosphorus, and potassium.

The nitrogen, phosphorus, and potassium in these animals' manure are extremely beneficial to plant growth. Additionally, they are an excellent source of calcium, which is necessary for plant growth.

It is important to consider that some chickens will eat many seeds, thus reducing the yield you receive or killing it altogether. This can be combated by purchasing organic feed for your poultry. The same process can be applied to rabbits as well; however, their droppings tend to be larger than chickens' droppings, which is where the problem stems from.

Soil health plays a critical role in sustainable gardening. It can be a fun project for gardeners who are environmentally conscious and want to do their part in protecting their environment. Healthy soil is aesthetically pleasing, but it is also a necessity for good plant growth.

CHAPTER 10: COMPOST

Composting breaks down organic matter and turns it into nutrient-rich soil for your plants. It's a natural process that has been going on for millennia, albeit usually without the help of humans. Composting is among the most effective ways to improve your soil while also reusing or recycling the many waste materials that most people discard - but not you.

Sustainable gardening and composting go hand in hand. Compost is one of the healthiest soils you can have, and it's very easy to make at home. It's also good for your household waste and leaves you with much less to take out the garbage each week.

You don't have to own a lot of land to compost - not even a yard. If you have any plot of land at all - no matter how small - you can compost, there. You can also start immediately if you have a kitchen compost pile, free from large items like pots and pans.

Components of a successful and healthy compost

To ensure your compost is healthy and free from disease, you need to make sure it has all the following vital components:

Right material

The compost needs to have a balance of different materials:

1. Green matter

This is the fresh material, such as leaves and grass clippings. It is full of energy and should be used quickly so that it doesn't decay in the open air and release greenhouse gases. The green matter should make up about 50% of your compost.

2. Brown matter

Brown matter is material that has already started to decay, such as wood chips or dried leaves, straw, newspaper, and cardboard. This type of material takes much longer to decompose than green matter, but it provides a carbon source for microbes to use. It should account for about 40% of your compost pile.

3. Water-rich material

The best water-rich materials are kitchen scraps and animal manure (if you are using it), but anything moist will do - except lawn clippings, which will leave your heap smelling bad without adding microbes. The best water-rich materials should make up about 20% of your compost.

4. Other matter

You might want to add some manure, shredded paper, or anything else lying around in your house. To expedite the composting process, avoid adding an excessive amount at once, as it will take significantly longer to decompose than the other components mentioned previously. The best matter to include is kitchen scraps and animal manure if you are using them. The best if you are not using either one is shredded paper or cardboard, which are excellent water-binders. The other items should make up about 5% of your compost.

The last matter you should consider adding is a lot of woodchips or sawdust, as these will help bind materials together in your compost. However, avoid including any dry material such as tree branches, leaves, and dead grass or weeds. If you add an excessive amount of this type of material to your compost heap, you risk creating a huge mess.

You want to keep the heap moist, but not too moist to the point where it is wetter than your unmixed brown and dark black (finished) compost pile - which shouldn't be more than 80% full. The finished compost should be at least 60-80% full since it has all been broken down and the excess has been removed.

Right temperature

One of the most common mistakes of new composters is failing to monitor the temperature of their compost heap. A compost pile should be maintained at a temperature between 58-70 degrees Fahrenheit but not too hot; it shouldn't get hotter than 90 degrees Fahrenheit or colder than 32 degrees Fahrenheit.

The compost pile should be kept with plenty of airflows and good drainage - near the center of your yard, where the wind will move the pile around. Each morning you want to turn over your compost, remove any material that has settled down into the bottom of the heap, and added rotors to your compost. Also, add more brown and green materials during this time. It would be beneficial if you repeated the exercise at night, or at least once a day.

If the pile gets too hot, you will have a problem with pathogens, which will spread to the plants you grow with your compost. Too cold, and it will take your compost longer to break down. Ideally, composting should happen between June and October when there are long days and not so many cold nights. Your compost can break down faster before the winter sets in.

You might want to consider placing your pile in something that shields it from the wind if it's not in the center of your yard. You could also add a tarp to the top of your pile if it's outdoors, which will hold the heat in and protect it from the rain. This way, you should be able to maintain a temperature between 58-70 degrees Fahrenheit.

Right balance of microbes

Microbes are single-celled organisms that help break down organic materials. In a healthy compost heap, you will find many different microbes, many of which are beneficial to your garden.

Very few people understand the importance of microbes in a compost pile. The reason for this is that few people make a compost heap. Composting is also one of the most misunderstood processes in gardening. Many factors can affect a compost pile, including lack of air, too much air, and good air circulation.

You should not dump all your kitchen waste into a compost pile. It's better, to begin with, the easier items like fruit and vegetable peels, eggshells, and coffee grounds first so that you can experience composting at your own pace before dumping everything else into your heap at once.

Microbes like a moist environment, so you're best to keep your compost heap moist. Make it a habit to sprinkle some water on the compost heap every day if it begins to dry out.

Your compost should ideally have a ratio of 50:1 or 40:1 microbe to non-microbes (dry matter). Still, you can adjust this ratio by adding more moisture or dry materials, as both will stimulate the growth of bacteria and fungi (microbes).

All gardeners know that plants need rich nutrition from the soil to be healthy and productive. Microbes are no exception. They can also produce plant nutrients such as nitrogen, phosphorus, sulfur compounds, and essential B vitamins.

To expedite the composting process, you can incorporate some animal manure into your heap. Manure is a wonderful source of microbes, and it has a generous amount of nitrogen. But be sure that you don't use any fresh manure since this can cause odors and attract vermin.

Organic matter such as leaves is also very beneficial in your compost pile, and they are a great way to get started. They are available almost all year round - which means a continuous supply of friendly microbes - and they don't have to be broken down or mixed with anything else.

To get the best results from your microbes, adding some nitrogen-rich materials is a good idea, such as grass clippings or kitchen scraps. These have a high moisture content, making them perfect for attracting microbes.

If you want to add animal manure or other organic matter to your compost heap, mix it with leaves or other dry material to encourage microbes. If you add a large handful of manure to your compost pile without thoroughly mixing it in, the pile will take much longer to decompose than if the two are properly mixed.

Composting can seem like a daunting task to the beginner, but if you learn to pay attention to the key factors of composting, it should not be too hard for you to do it at home. You can also check if your local municipality has a composting program.

If you compost your materials at home, you will soon discover that composting is an easy way to reduce the amount of trash. In addition, you will gain richer soil for your garden and save yourself money on fertilizer!

CHAPTER 11: COMPANION GARDENING

Companion planting is an old gardening methodology, especially for vegetables. This practice involves planting two or more different plants near each other to derive some benefit from their proximity.

This benefit could be increased growth, increased yield, pest repellency, or attraction of predators of common pests. While scientific research may not always corroborate folklore about companion planting, it does add diversity to the garden, which may help reduce problems and increase yields and flavor.

Elaborate combinations

There is a wide range of companion planting regimes based on different regions' varying beliefs and observations. One practice involves many plants that have a symbiotic relationship with each other, taking the place of fertilizers or pesticides. These relationships involve nitrogen-fixing bacteria, insects that help control pests, or some combination of this and other mechanisms.

Some examples are:

1. Tomatoes and marigold

A study published in science found that interplanting marigolds with tomatoes significantly reduces infestation by the tomato hornworm, a major pest of tomato plants and the larvae of a hawk moth.

The researchers planted four tomato plants, each surrounded by four marigolds, every 15 inches in a square plot. They then placed small pieces of cardboard on the ground around each plant. Within 24 hours, it was clear that the cardboard attracted egg-laying female moths of the hawkmoth, and their offspring fed on the marigold flowers and leaves, avoiding tomatoes.

This simple technique reduces populations of this destructive pest by approximately 90 percent and is especially useful for home gardeners who do not want to spray poisons on their food crops.

2. Carrots and lettuce

Research published in the Agronomy Journal (2012) found that planting carrots near lettuce helped reduce the number of carrot root flies. Carrot fly eggs are laid in the soil, and the larvae feed on the roots of carrots. The larvae then pupate, emerging as adult flies attracted to carrot plants.

The researchers found that when about 30 small lettuce plants were planted within a 10-foot radius of each carrot plant, fewer than 3 percent of carrot root flies emerged from their eggs. If a single large lettuce plant was located nearby, no flies came from the eggs when tested over two weeks.

3. Garlic and potatoes

Several studies have shown that planting potatoes near garlic and brassicas reduces the number of pests and the need for fungicides. For example, a study in Australia (2005) found that using garlic with four different varieties of potatoes reduced the number of potato tuberworm by 15-25 percent. In another study (2010), the same researchers found that garlic reduced infestation by potato cyst nematodes by more than 90 percent.

Other studies have found that planting brassicas near potatoes reduce the amount of fusarium wilt, a serious disease that can infect potatoes, tomatoes, peppers, and eggplants. The roots of these plants have symbiotic bacteria that produce chemicals to kill the fungi.

Carrots and parsnips help protect beets from two types of nematodes, and radishes do the same for cabbage worms.

4. Sweet potatoes and onions

Planting these two plants near each other helps reduce populations of seed-eating grubs in sweet potato roots. In Central America, the research found that planting one-and two-year-old sweet potatoes with green tops within a 15-inch radius of onion plants reduced the number of onions damaged by seed-eating grubs. The onion plants also benefited from the proximity of their neighbors, as they were healthier and had less disease than those planted away from other plants.

5. Garlic and onions

This works similarly to the previous companion planting combination, but with garlic rather than sweet potatoes.

The research published in 2009 found that planting one garlic plant within 15 feet of each of four onion plants reduced the damage caused by white-rot fungus in the onions by 50 percent. Additionally, it inhibited the spread of certain fungal diseases on garlic during dry periods, most notably during the winter, when there is insufficient moisture in the soil for fungi to survive.

6. Garlic and tomatoes

Planting garlic at the base of tomatoes reduces damage caused by slugs caught in the tomato residue, which prevents them from reaching higher levels in the plant to feed on leaf tissue. To be effective, garlic must be planted within 15 inches of tomato plants because it grows very close to the ground and is protected from damage by briers and other weeds that otherwise threaten it. Its odor also causes slugs to avoid it.

This combination also works well with potatoes, which can increase yields significantly when planted next to garlic (with or without potatoes) to provide a more stable food source for the slugs.

7. Sunflowers and squash

Sunflowers attract aphids, which are a common pest of squash plants. The research published in HortScience (2001) found that intercropping sunflowers with squash reduced the number of aphids on squash by 8 percent compared to a control plot where no sunflowers were planted. This is because natural predators remove the aphids in the sunflowers, and those that move to the squash are controlled by parasitoids.

8. Mushroom and strawberries

Planting strawberries next to mushrooms stimulates the growth of the mushroom mycelium, which encourages increased production of chemicals that repel slugs and deter other pests. The result is that strawberry plants are more resistant to diseases and insect damage, and the strawberries themselves are healthier and produce more fruit. The University of Illinois found that planting mushrooms five feet in front of strawberry plants increased their yield by 60 percent. This is because the chemicals produced by the mycelium are not just used by the host plant but also spread to neighboring plants.

Unfortunately, some companion plantings do not benefit the garden as much as others.

Some plants do better when grown alone and not near a companion plant.

1. Corn and pole beans

The corn pollen from the corn plants interferes with the pollination of neighboring pole bean plants, which are in flower at approximately the same time. In addition, pole beans may be killed by the sooty mold fungus that grows on neighboring corn leaves. Intercropping corn and beans, according to research conducted by the Ontario Ministry of Agriculture and Food, results in plants that are 20% smaller and produce 30% less grain than plants grown alone. Planting bonemeal between corn and beans helps encourage plant growth. Still, it does not improve pollination because there is no difference between the amount of protein produced in plants grown with or without bonemeal.

2. Potatoes and sweet potatoes

Sweet potatoes are not compatible with other root crops such as potatoes, turnips, carrots, or beets because their roots give off a toxin called dicarboximide when they contact other roots growing nearby. Planting bonemeal between corn and beans helps encourage plant growth. Still, it does not improve pollination because there is no difference between the amount of protein produced in plants grown with or without bonemeal.

3. Peas with potatoes

The peas are poisonous to potatoes and cause damage by giving off a gas called indole acetic acid into the potato tubers. When there is little or no soil around the pea roots, the gas escapes into the air and can harm insects that meet them (including bees), not people. The production of this gas is stimulated by an enzyme produced in the roots of nearby plants. These include radishes, cabbage, broccoli, Brussels sprouts, and cauliflower - all of which are compatible with potatoes. Researchers from Cornell University suspected that they produce less gas when soil is around these roots than if there is no soil nearby.

4. Carrots with beans

The soil around the carrot roots is toxic to beans, which can cause the roots to swell and die. There were two other root crops close to the carrots— beets and onions— . Still, both are also compatible with potatoes, so there is no need for a gas barrier other than between peas and potatoes, as recommended above.

5. Carrots with cabbage

Carrots compete for nitrogen fertilizer, but so does cabbage, which has a greater absorption rate from the soil. The analysis of this partnership suggests that for best results, keep the two plants at least 12 inches apart to prevent competition between them for nitrogen from crop residues in certain situations.

6. Carrots with rutabagas

Rutabagas have a very large taproot, which can interfere with the growth of nearby carrots. The analysis of this partnership suggests that for best results, keep the two plants at least 12 inches apart to prevent competition between them for nitrogen from crop residues in certain situations. Soil type and moisture are factors to consider as well.

7. Onion with broccoli

Broccoli is vulnerable to a disease known as root maggots, which live in the soil around onions but not in sandy or loamy soils where this combination is often planted. Crop rotation is the favored solution, but careful use of pesticides can help deal with the problem. Although there is no reason that broccoli and onions cannot be grown together in the same garden, they should be separated by at least thirty feet to avoid harmful side effects.

8. Beans with tomatoes

Bean roots are poisonous to tomato plants, and beans will also compete for water and fertilizer with tomatoes, making this combination poor for most gardeners.

This may be an issue when tomatoes are grown in containers since the soil will not be sterilized between plants to prevent diseases from spreading between them. Thoroughly disinfecting the area where you plan to plant your container garden before you do so will reduce the chances that diseases will spread from one plant to another.

Knowing which plants are compatible with each other and which are not is the first step in planning your garden. Take advantage of this information to create an attractive, productive garden that will provide you with many years of gardening pleasure. Sustainable gardens can be created with companion planting.

CHAPTER 12: HARVESTING AND BEYOND

Harvesting is something we all must do eventually. You might be surprised at how much you can harvest and how little space. What will we do with the remaining harvest? There are plenty of options available, and this chapter will explore some of the most popular.

1. Own consumption

The easiest way to get rid of extra produce is to eat it yourself. This is a great idea for certain foods that store well, such as onions and potatoes. But some things are not the best tasting when eaten fresh, like green squash.

There are a lot of options to prolong freshness. Some of these are discussed below:

Canning

Canning is probably the best method for preserving your produce. Several different types of food, including fruits and vegetables, meats, fish, and even jams and jellies can be canned. This is a very popular option for those who are particularly adept in the kitchen or are interested in cooking. Canning is the process of boiling food in glass jars with a food-grade sealant to preserve it for later use.

Canning your harvest
Materials:

- Container (large, wide-mouth pint jar works well)
- Sterilizing tools (screwturner, canning tongs, lid lifter)

- Headspace jigger
- Jar lifter
- Ball and stick thermometer
- Canning jar funnel/pint pot/jar with lid ring on top of the jar for filling jars with hot water to use as a weight during canning.

Process:

Step 1: Wash and sterilize the jars.

Wash your jars, inside and out, in hot, soapy water and put them on a rack to dry. To soften the rubber seal around the lids, place them in a pot of boiling water for 15 minutes. The lids don't need to be sterilized, but you should keep them in a pot of water.

Step 2: Make a filling layer for jars.

In a clean jar, put a tablespoon of white vinegar and a teaspoon of salt (to prevent bacterial growth). You will use this later to fill the jars with hot water, and to make sure that the food is completely covered in liquid during the canning process to kill off any bacteria that might be present. The leftover vegetables are called the "filling" layer. Later on, you will pour this over your food once it's processed to make sure the food is completely covered in liquid during the canning process to kill off any bacteria that might be present.

Step 3: Get your vegetables ready.

Wash your vegetables and cut them up into small pieces or slices. You can also blanch veggies before adding them to the jar to make sure they are nice and clean and to remove any strong flavors, but this isn't necessary.

Step 4: Put the food in jars with the filling layer.

Using a jar funnel, fill each jar halfway with food and then add a tablespoon of white vinegar followed by a teaspoon of salt over the top (this will not only keep your food preserved better but will also keep it tasting fresh) and then fill the jar to the top with the filling liquid.

Step 5: Close jars and seal.

Put the lids on with a ring and screw them down until tight. Then, a hot water bath is processed for about 10 minutes to ensure that you have properly killed off any bacteria living in your food. Process for 5 minutes for jams or jellies, and 20-25 minutes for everything else. This can be done by working in batches, but make sure that all your jars are processed at once so that they don't have time to cool down too much before being put into their canning bath.

Step 6: Remove.

Use a jar lifter and lid lifter to remove the jars from the canning bath. Allow 10 minutes for them to cool on a cooling rack or towel before removing the lids with tongs (careful not to tip the jars over) and storing them for future use.

Preserving

Apart from canning, there are numerous other methods of food preservation, each with its own set of advantages and disadvantages.

These are the most common options:

Freezing

Freezing your food is a great option for things that don't last long, such as sliced fruit or cooked foods. However, when freezing fruits, you need to make sure that they are completely raw to prevent any off flavors. This means not adding any sugar or honey or syrups or anything else that will prevent them from freezing well. However, when it comes to veggies and other items, it's best to blanch them first in boiling water for about 3 minutes before putting them in the freezer (this process is called par blanching) to prevent any off flavors.

Dehydrating

You can either dehydrate your food in the sun or with an electric dehydrator. Once dehydrated, your food will lose its moisture and become leathery, dry, and brittle. This is a great way to keep foods with a lot of water content (such as fruits) but does not work well for veggie preservation because the chemical breakdown changes their color, flavor, and structure. So, this kind of preservation would not be ideal for veggies like cucumbers or zucchini squash. It would be great for things like tomatoes and apples, however. You can also use this option to make your beef jerky or fruit leather.

Salting/Brining

Salt is a very popular food preservative because it kills bacteria without negatively affecting the flavor of your food. Salt draws moisture from the food and inhibits the growth of bacteria. Salting your food should be done in moderation, or it will draw out too much moisture and make your food mushy. Therefore, fruits that contain a lot of water, like strawberries, shouldn't be salted until they're fully dried (and even then, only 1/2 teaspoon of salt per quart of fruit). Brining is a great option for meat preservation because it pulls moisture out of the meat without removing desirable flavors. However, the brine must be neutral so that no desirable flavors are removed. This can be accomplished by using a vinegar-salt solution rather than straight salt.

You can use this process in many ways. You can salt food overnight (or leave it in a salt cure for a few days) and then refrigerate them, or you could put the food in brine for several days and then refrigerate it. Brining is very similar to pickling; except it's done with hot water rather than vinegar. This preserves foods by adding moisture and making sure that the salt goes down inside the meat (like pickles) and not just on the surface.

2. Sell

Selling your product is a great way to get added income while preserving the fruits of your labor. There are many ways to sell your crops: farmers' markets, farm stands, or even through local or online stores.

Farmers' Markets

Farmers' markets are a great way to sell products because they provide a sense of community and allow customers to speak directly with the farmers who grew their food. It's also more convenient for people looking for fresh, local ingredients because many of these markets do not require you to pre-order what you will be selling like online stores do and instead require that you come down with whatever you have on hand at the time (make sure that you bring enough for everyone) as well as making sure that your crop is at least ripe. Many farms stand at farmers' markets and have a great selection of fruits and vegetables, so you are sure to have something for everyone in the family to choose from.

Farm Stands

While farmers' markets are an excellent venue for selling your products, a farm stand can help you maximize your harvest. You won't have to worry about pre-ordering or people stealing your ingredients if you do it this way; instead, you can do it whenever you want and at whatever price you want. However, this also means that this is not as much of a community atmosphere, and there is a greater chance of people trying to steal your food from you because they can do so anonymously. In addition, farm stands tend to be more expensive than farmers' markets (but for excellent reasons) so if you can do both, then do so.

3. Participate in CSAs

Participating in a CSA is also a great way to sell your product because it allows you to do so without the hassle of running a farm stand. Community Supported Agriculture, or CSA, is a type of co-op in which members purchase a share of the farm's harvest at the start of the season and then receive weekly deliveries (typically weekly). These deliveries will contain everything that has been grown on that week's harvest and recipes and tips for things that can be made from whatever has been delivered (including the items that you have fresh from the Farm).

A CSA is a great way to sell products because it allows you to do so without the hassle of running a farm stand.

Harvesting the fruits of your labor is rewarding, but there are times when you have an excess of produce, and you know that you can't possibly eat it all up. Whether you harvest your crops yourself or not, many people do not know what to do with all the unwanted produce they may have after a growing season ends. Fortunately, there are many options available, each of which is sure to give you a great way to help finance your next growing season and create some awesome food.

CHAPTER 13: GARDENING AND HEALTH

Gardening is an excellent way to maintain an active lifestyle, alleviate stress, and reconnect with nature. Gardening can provide enjoyment for people of all ages and abilities, including children. It's a healthy hobby that requires physical activity in the fresh air outdoors and produces fruits and vegetables in our kitchens.

The garden is a natural place to find relaxation from the stresses of life — like your job or family life. Gardeners are outside people by definition! Gardeners need lots of sunlight and enjoy being out of doors in all types of weather. They work hard to plant gardens without pesticides or chemicals that could harm them and the environment. Gardeners are educated by necessity because they learn about the earth, water, sunlight, and insects and how to work with all those elements for the garden's good.

Benefits of Gardening in Health

1. Physical movement

A person usually must move around to plant, weed, and water the garden. Gardening is a good way to stay active and exercise your body. Gardening helps to keep the heart healthy. Gardening requires using different muscles, which burn calories and can help you lose weight if you do it regularly. The New Zealand Medical Journal (2020) has shown that gardening is a low-impact exercise that can help fight heart disease and diabetes. Gardening is the perfect exercise for people with heart conditions or people who are overweight since it doesn't strain the joints. This could result in lower blood pressure and a decrease in cholesterol.

2. Emotional health

Gardening can help improve your emotional health because it provides good opportunities to explore your emotions. A study by Cornell University showed that people who garden experience higher happiness levels and improved quality of life. It is shown that the brain produces a chemical called endorphin when a person is involved in an outdoor activity. The pituitary gland produces endorphins, which help a person feel happy or pleasurable. Gardening can be one of those activities that can create an emotional high for someone who has a lot of stress, anxiety, and depression.

3. Meditation

If you meditate, gardening can provide a great way to relax and feel more at peace. Gardening provides an outdoor place free from all the distractions of modern civilization. When you are a part of nature, your senses become sharper and more in tune with your surroundings.

Leisure activities such as gardening are relaxing to both the body and mind. Gardeners don't need any special training to enjoy the benefits of sunlight and fresh air. Gardening can provide a different kind of relaxation or stress relief than other leisure activities, including reading a book or watching TV on a couch.

Gardening provides the opportunity to take a break from the stress of modern life. Gardening promotes good relationships with nature, and it feels good to "return" to a natural state of being. Nature is also a good exercise because it engages your muscles and helps you burn calories.

4. Play

Gardening provides a great way to play. Playing is an emotional release that helps you work through problems and release frustrations. Playing makes your mind more active, and it encourages the body. Gardening provides a mental break from other activities, which refreshes the mind, allowing you to think more clearly and make better decisions.

Gardening provides a great way to release stress by playing in the garden. Playing can be a fun activity, or it can be a therapeutic release for emotions. Playing can be a source of stress relief, which everybody needs.

5. Socializing

According to Cornell University, gardening can provide meaningful social interactions for people who garden. This study found that socializing with other people fosters happiness and improves your quality of life. Other studies have also shown that gardening is a good way to meet new people and make new friends in your community.

The Cornell study showed that many gardeners had made new friends by volunteering in community gardens, so it can help you meet different people in your area. Gardening provides a great time for sharing stories and bonding with others who share the same interest as you do.

The benefits of gardening don't stop once you have picked your last tomato or harvested the last head of lettuce. The garden itself provides ongoing relaxation, satisfaction, and pleasure for those who take time out to enjoy it. You can enjoy the garden any time you want, by just opening the back door or walking around your property. Gardening is a good activity for any age, and there are many benefits to gardening.

CHAPTER 14: REGENERATIVE GARDENING

Regenerative gardening is a type of permaculture gardening that integrates ecology and hydrology to create greater species diversity. The aim is to grow as many edible plants as possible while growing the soil. It's all about creating more life, not just on your plate but all around you.

Regenerative gardening means creating various habitats for the many different species that are a part of your garden. This concept embodies helping mother nature through adding biodiversity, increasing water retention, and building soil fertility. It is an ecological approach to gardening that aims for sustainability.

A regenerative garden is a three-part system:

1. Front edge

Contains annual vegetable crops and perennial vegetables and herbs. These plants help provide food for the soil organisms and contribute to building a healthy ecosystem. Annual vegetables are usually harvested and replaced with a new crop every year. But perennial vegetables and herbs do not get harvested, prolonging their life in the garden, and regenerating the soil over time.

2. Middle layer

Contains perennial crops such as fruit trees, shrubs, and berry crops. This helps lay the foundation for soil fertility and water retention by adding organic matter to the soil every year through its leaves and roots.

3. Back edge

Contains a mixture of fruits, herbs, and soil building plants like veggie garden crops, complementary plants to perennial crops, and soil improvers. These are plants that add nutrients to the soil or improve water retention. They also contribute organic matter to the soil by decomposing organic matter in the root zone.

The three parts of a regenerative garden can be planted together in any way you desire. In some cases, you may choose to grow just one type of plant from each section (for example, only a fruit tree from the front edge), while other times, you may want your entire garden to follow this concept.

Practicing regenerative gardening

Regenerative gardening can be done on any scale (from an apartment balcony to a backyard). A lot of the time, the difference between regenerative design and traditional gardening is a long-term attitude. Traditional gardens are usually steeped in one season and then pulled out when the season is over. Regenerative gardens last for many years, with individual parts replanted annually or even every few years.

Key components of a regenerative garden

1. Soil fertility

Building soil fertility means adding organic matter to your garden's compost, mulch, and other compostable materials. These materials help increase the mineral content in your soil and add beneficial microbes and aerobic activity to the soil.

2. Water retention

Building water retention means creating a system that can absorb and hold onto water for longer than traditional garden beds. This protects plants from stress or suffering in times of drought while also preventing runoff contamination into nearby ponds and waterways. Soil layers like mulches, composts, or manure can create deep watering zones that allow plants' roots to reach down into them when they need moisture.

3. Enhanced biodiversity

Creating a diversity of species in your garden can increase how your garden naturally regenerates itself. This is partly due to the increased diversity of species that occur because of growing in this type of garden, as well as the increased food available to their predators. When numerous species coexist, they can compete for scarce resources such as sunlight, water, and space, resulting in increased growth and productivity.

Regenerative gardens can play an important role in preserving biodiversity due to their ability to mimic nature's ecosystem closely. They make a lot of use of perennial plants, which are plants that live longer and have more time to be productive. They also use perennials that flower and bear fruit before dying or being harvested, which means more food for pollinators and beneficial insects in the garden. The presence of these flowers attracts beneficial insects such as bees, butterflies, and moths which come to pollinate the garden and assist with pest control.

How to practice regenerative gardening

Step 1: Choose plants for your front edge according to the topography of your garden

Regenerative gardens need various plants to provide services and food for a long period. For example, you might want to grow a vegetable on the front edge that is better suited to the hot summers while also growing a fruit tree in this area that flowers and bears fruit early, and ready to be harvested by the time summer hits.

Step 2: Add organic material to your soil's surface

Organic matter adds more moisture retention to the soil and improves its structure by improving soil aeration It also helps with alleviating compaction, which prevents water from percolating into the soil instead causing it to run off into storm drains and waterways.

Step 3: Plant your garden according to how you want it to look

When the season is over, you can pull out the plants in your garden. All the roots and leaves will go back into the ground, decomposing and replenishing the soil with nutrients. A great thing about this is that you do not have to use as much fertilizer, and all your organic matter will stay in place. This means that you also do not have to use chemical fertilizers, which can hurt soil organisms and provide exposure to harmful chemicals like pesticides if used.

Step 4: Monitor your garden's health and make necessary changes accordingly.

In a traditional garden, soil fertility is often decreased after a season because the soil is depleted of nutrients. In contrast, regenerative gardens replenish their soils with organic matter every year, which leads to increased fertility at the end of the season. Leaf colors can indicate that your plants are doing well, but it can also indicate that something is wrong with your garden and that you should address it right away. For example, if the plants all suffer from nutrient deficiencies or insect infestation, you know that something needs to change, and you should act.

Step 5: Go to Step 1!

You can repeat this cycle for as long as you want.

Regenerative gardening is a simple concept that can be applied to any garden. It involves using the right tool for the job so that you can improve soil fertility, water retention, and biodiversity while saving time and money.

The regeneration process will lead to a thriving garden that requires less maintenance and yields a higher harvest. This way, you will have more time to spend and enjoy in your garden while also being able to keep it alive indefinitely.

Regenerative gardening is a long-term practice involving several steps. Still, with the right information, it can be achieved even by those who are new to gardening or have always struggled with keeping their garden alive.

CHAPTER 15: GARDEN JOURNALING

Garden journaling is a great way to keep track of planting dates, pests and survivors, blooming plants, etc. Journaling can bring a rare kind of satisfaction to journalers, as they see their plantings unfold day by day.

Documenting your garden's progress day by day is a great way to stay on top of your garden's development.

Benefits of keeping a gardening journal

1. Schedule for plant rotation

A big area of gardening success is learning to grow plants in different areas each year. By keeping a journal, you can see what worked and what didn't in your garden from year to year. There will be entries for the last few years' gardens so you can learn from your mistakes and draw conclusions based on the successes and failures of previous years.

2. Schedule for pruning or fertilizing

Most of us don't have time to do everything at once. That's where journaling comes in handy. Write down when you fertilize your plants and which fertilizer you used. Most plants need to be pruned after the first year to promote healthy growth the following spring. Journaling will give you a clear picture of when to perform these important details to do them correctly and on time.

3. When, what you planted

Nothing is more aggravating than forgetting what you planted the year before. When you journal, you can write down when each plant was cultivated and where and what was planted in each section. By looking back through your journal, you'll remember exactly what went into your garden the previous year.

4. Monitor weather

You can document the weather for each day in your garden journal. This information will help you when preparing your garden for the coming season. You'll be able to determine if you should water your garden, how much rain you should expect, and what kind of plants will fare best when it snows.

5. Troubleshooting your garden

This is a great section to use to figure out what's wrong with your plants. Journaling will help you quickly identify the problems so that they can be corrected before they seriously affect your garden.

6. Milestones

This is a good way to keep track of your yearly achievements. Write down how many plants you grew, how much money you spent on the garden, etc. Once a year, you'll be able to look back on your accomplishments and see how far you've come since the previous year.

7. Plant profiles and vendors

If you're not sure what plants to buy for your garden, write down each plant's name and contact information. This is also a good way to keep track of the contacts you use for each order. You will find this information as you record in your gardening journal.

8. Achievements and goals for the garden

You can keep track of the gardening activities you pursue and your goals and achievements for each season. You can include this information in your gardening journal. At the end of each year, you will have at least one year's worth of information to refer to and review as needed.

Types of gardening journaling: Bullet journal

There are various types of gardening journaling out there depending on what type of gardening you like to do or if you want to keep a public record about your garden and how it is doing each season.

The Bullet journal is one of the most popular gardening journals because it is very versatile for any gardener. The Bullet journal was originated by Ryder Carroll, who created a different kind of notebook where you can put in as many pages as needed. Because there are no pre-planned layouts, you can make your layout that suits your needs and doesn't have to follow the traditional book layout. The Bullet Journal is also beneficial because you can add anything that you want to your page so that it doesn't have to be as pre-planned. This makes the Bullet journal very flexible and usable in any situation or situation.

Using a bullet journal for gardening

Bullet journaling is used for many different forms of gardening; it can be helpful to note down the things that you want to do or want to try or what you want to add to your garden. Bullet journaling can help you track where your garden has been and how it's growing each season. Keeping track of your plants and their growth will help you know when a plant is ready for harvest or if it isn't growing or doing well because of pests. You may also keep track of pest problems in specific areas where plants are dying to see what kind of pest it is that is causing the problem and how to fix it before it gets out of hand.

Things to consider when starting a bullet journal

If you are new to using bullet journaling, you should keep in mind the important things to ensure that you understand how to use a bullet journal for gardening.

1. Supplies

The first thing is to ensure that you have all your supplies or what is needed for your garden. This includes paper and envelopes, planners or notebooks, pens and pencils, and any other items necessary for gardening, such as fertilizer or pesticides. Additionally, you should be familiar with the various types of pages that can be included in your bullet journals, including checklists, lists, headers, and dividers.

2. Plan your garden journal

After assembling all your supplies, create the bullet journal layout that works best for you. If you want to put in checklists or if you don't want to add a header each time, then a horizontal layout might work better for what needs to be tracked. If there are certain things that you want to keep track of regularly, then having a monthly calendar layout with weekly boxes for the days will be best, so it's easy for you to track and see what is going on each day.

3. Use your journal

The last thing to consider when starting a bullet garden journal is adding the pages and using them. You should make notes about what is going on with your garden, what plants you have started, or if there are any pests that you want to keep an eye on. The Bullet journal can be helpful in many ways, depending on what you need it for. Keeping track of your garden each day will help you see what's growing, any problems or new plants that have come up, or if the plant has stopped growing because of a pest problem.

Using Bullet Journal Techniques to Create a Garden Journal
1. Select a Journal for Your Use

Any open book will suffice. If you're new to journaling, look for something with lines, grids, or dotted grids. Choose something you like but isn't too fancy, as it will be taken into the garden and likely become dirty and wet. You can also choose a sketchbook or composition book.

2. Setting Up Your Journal

You can use the pre-printed pages that come with a sketchbook or composition book or create your charts and calendars. The first few pages of your journal can be used to keep track of information about yourself, such as how many times you go into the garden each week, what kind of plants you like to grow, and what kinds of flowers you like best. You can also keep track of different gardening techniques used in previous years and which ones worked best for you. This will help keep track of where your garden has been so it won't have any problems from the previous year in the next year. You should write down any problems you have had with your garden or what was done to fix a problem. Many people like to write down any new plants or vegetables that they have in their garden so that it can help them see what is working best for the plant. If there is a problem or pest, they can write down what they are doing to fix the problem, and if it works, you know what to do if the same thing happens again. While brief notes are beneficial, feel free to elaborate to transfer ideas from your head to the paper. The critical step is to put them on paper.

3. Setting Up Information and Keeping Track

Each square of your daily journal should have a writing space, with additional space under the writing space if needed. Start at the top and bottom of the page. Set up information that you want to track each day. For example, write "Plant" in one square, then write the plant name, what you've done, who did it, when you did it, and in what order you did it. After that, start over again so that there are no duplicates. Number each day of the week at the top of the page to keep track of what day of the week it is in your journal.

4. Keeping Track After That

Continue doing this for each page. The next page can be for insects, pests, or weeds that need to be taken care of and what you did to take care of them. Keep working your way through your journal. You can keep track on every single page if you want to by writing "Keep Track" on each square, or you can stay at the top and bottom of the pages and only write down important things that need to be taken care of, such as weeding or watering, or if you want to enter information about what type of plant or plant it is that needs to be taken care of.

Information you can track in your garden journal should include:

Daily

How many times did you go into the garden, who went with you, what were the temperatures and humidity (this will help keep track of any problems that could damage your plants), who watered the plants and how they were watered, and if you had any problems or pests? You can also write down what kind of flowers or plants are planted or growing in the garden, which insects are on them, which pests should be looked at, what types of organic fertilizers you use (you can add a rating for your plants or flowers), when you are weeding or watering the garden and any other information that is needed.

Monthly

How many plants have died, how many weeds have come up, and other important information about the garden?

Annual and Seasonal

How much water was used in the garden and how much rain was received, and how often did you spray the plants with pesticides or what did you spray with? Anything else that needs to be measured can be added to the information in these categories. Each column can be filled out in this fashion as needed.

5. Use the Journal for History

The journal can be used for planting information, after planting information, watering information, and pest control or weed control information. You should put this information in the top left corner of each page as a guide and reference whenever you look at your journal.

All of this can be accomplished in one book, and all you need to do is place it in a prominent location or bring it into the garden with you to ensure that you don't forget any critical information that may need to be addressed in your garden.

CONCLUSION

Sustainable gardening is a way of planting and caring for plants that takes natural resources and keeps them in the ground to grow future crops. It's a way of living without harming people or the ecosystem.

Planning your garden is important for a successful harvest. It can mean the difference between a vegetable garden full of beautiful crops that taste great, and one choked with weeds and plants that don't produce.

Sustainable gardening is about producing food for yourself or your community as naturally as possible. It's about becoming more self-sufficient, it's about growing healthy plants, and it's about saving money! Sustainable gardening takes some work to get started, but you will find that your garden will produce great-tasting food without chemicals or pesticides once you get the hang of it.

Many gardening types are both for your backyards or in a small space.

You can successfully grow something of use for yourself, for your community or for someone in need with good planning and organization.

You may be planting a small vegetable garden on some property that belongs to a friend or neighbor. It may be a plot of land you have purchased for your own.

Many considerations go into a garden plan, and there are several different types of gardens to choose from.

All plants need certain things to grow to be healthy and strong. Some plants require different care, like hot or dry soil or wet and cool temperatures.

It's good to do some research on what types of plants you would like to grow in your garden. You can use the internet and search through websites that tell you what each type of plant likes or doesn't like. You can even ask a local nursery to give you a list of plants they would recommend for the area you live in.

When planning your garden, it's important to know how much space you have available for planting. If you are planting a large garden, you may want to think about how you will get it into a usable space. If you are only planting a small plot, you may want to consider how you will make the space look nice.

You need to consider the soil in your yard or garden and what plants you have chosen to plant. Each different type of soil needs a different type of care and watering. Some plants like sandy soil, while others like moist soil. You will need to make sure that your plants have moisture and nutrients, so scout out the location of your garden and see what type of landscape will be suitable for your garden's variety of plants.

A watering system may not be necessary if you live in an area where natural rainfall occurs. But it will be a necessity if you live in a region where natural water is scarce. Think about how much water your garden needs and the best way to get it.

Growing seedlings is an essential part of gardening. Seedlings are small plants that you have started from seeds. Your seedlings are a little bit harder than seeds and can easily be transplanted into your garden, but not all plants can become seedlings, so make sure you figure out which ones the seeds you have will be able to grow into.

All seeds require three things to germinate: climate, moisture, and air. You must have all three of these things for your seedlings to grow well and produce a healthy plant that will give you a good harvest when the time comes.

There are a lot of growing mediums in which you can plant your seeds. The medium will depend on what plants you plan to grow and what type of diet they need to grow best. Some plants need rich soil with a lot of nutrients. Other plants prefer less fertile soil with not as many nutrients. Ensure that your planting medium contains the correct nutrients for your plants and will help them thrive in their environment.

Gardening has a lot of benefits for our well-being and our community. It's an important part of a healthy lifestyle and can save us money in the long run.

Once you've mastered it, you may discover that you're enjoying your garden far more than you anticipated. Sustainable gardening is a way of growing that can help us keep the world healthy and happy.

We need to learn how to create a better garden. We must learn about all these from designing the site, preparing the soil, planting and caring for plants properly, harvesting and processing the crops, organizing the plants, and finally, processing and preserving the crops. This requires time, effort, and study. We need to be patient and keep trying, and most importantly, having fun while gardening!

Call To Action

If you enjoyed this book , please share leave a review on amazon.

For more about gardening and being with a community of like-minded individuals please join our Facebook Group "Gardening For The Complete Beginner" and enter your email address to join in on the group. You can also get news for upcoming books from this publisher.

BIBLIOGRAPHY

https://www.nosoilsolutions.com/6-different-types-hydroponic-systems/

https://www.thespruce.com/apartment-gardening-for-beginners-4178600

https://www.trees.com/gardening-and-landscaping/nutrient-film-technique

https://www.thespruce.com/hydroponic-gardens-ebb-and-flow-systems-1939219

https://www.bhg.com/gardening/container/plans-ideas/vertical-gardening/

https://www.popularmechanics.com/home/how-to-plans/how-to/g847/how-to-start-a-vertical-garden/

https://www.seedsnow.com/blogs/news/best-time-to-plant-wheel

"Columbia Encyclopedia, Sixth Edition", 2017, Columbia University Press.

Harsley Agricultural Museum, "Vegetable Gardening: The Basics", ©2018

Excerpt from the "Harsley Agricultural Museum Collection" ©2018

http://www.publicworksinsight.com/water_supply/water_lines/pressure_lines.

Author: Sterling McDaniel (2012). "How to Install a Home-Made Drip Irrigation System". "Garden Tips".

www.davidsoutherndesignsllc.com/peeling-technique-video/

www.naturalgardeningforbeginnersguide.com/peeling-technique-video/

"The Encyclopedia of Seeds: Planter's Guide to Over 3,000 Traditional and Natural Plant Foods" by William Woys Weaver. University of California Press - 1974.

"Plant Physiology: Nutrient Effects on Biochemical Processes" by David Geiser and Luca Mazzoni. Sinauer Associates - 2004.

https://www.livingstonfuturefarmers.com/2014/03/09/how-to-grow-seedlings/

https://www.organicgardening.co.uk/features/growing_seedlings.asp

http://www.gardeningforabetterworld.com/growing-seedlings.html

http://www.gardenknowhow.com/plant-problems/pests/insects/how-to-get-rid-of-aphids.htm

http://extension.illinois.edu/veg/transplanting-seedlings-tips

http://www.gardenguides.com/4683/gardening-tips/all-about-transplanting-seedlings

https://www.chesshouseorganics.com/growing-in-coco-coir/

https://www.gardeningknowhow.com/edible/vegetables/vegetable-gardener/growing-coco-coir-organic-soil.

http://www.gardeners.com/how-to/garden-basics/how-to-make-compost

http://www.commonsensehome.com/composting/why_you_should_make_your_own

http://edis.ifas.ufl.edu/pdffiles/ES/es1875-1er.pdf

http://homeguides.sfgate.com/companion-planting-benefits-toxic-plants-91757.html

Printed in Great Britain
by Amazon

36789007R00155